EXECUTIVE Guide to
Preventing Information Technology Disasters

Springer
Berlin
Heidelberg
New York
Barcelona
Budapest
Hong Kong
London
Milan
Paris
Tokyo

Richard Ennals

EXECUTIVE
Guide to

Preventing Information Technology Disasters

 Springer

Richard Ennals
Professor of Business Information Technology
Kingston Business School
Kingston University
Kingston-upon-Thames
KT2 7LB

ISBN 3–540–19928–4 Springer-Verlag Berlin Heidelberg New York

British Library Cataloguing in Publication Data
Ennals, J. R.
  Executive Guide to Preventing
  Information Technology Disasters
  I. Title
  658.4038011
  ISBN   3–540–19928–4

Library of Congress Cataloging-in-Publication Data
Ennals, J. R. (John Richard), 1951–
  Executive guide to preventing information technology disasters / Richard Ennals.
    p.   cm.
  Includes bibliographical references and index.
  ISBN 3–540–19928–4 (pbk. : alk. paper)
  1. Information technology--Management.   2. Management information systems
  3. Computer security.   I. Title.
  T58.64.E66   1995
  658.4'78--dc20   95–30435

Interfaced from the author's disk by Geoff Amor
Typeset by Richard Powell Editorial and Production Services, Basingstoke, Hants RG22 4TX
Printed by Athenæum Press Ltd, Gateshead, England
34/3830-543210   (printed on acid-free paper)

Contents

Preface

As organisations become more dependent on information technology for their smooth running and their very survival, managers would like to find a guaranteed method of preventing IT disasters. This book argues that no such guarantee is possible, and that management in the age of IT has to consider the strengths and limitations of the technology, making appropriate use of human knowledge and skill.

An account is given of competing claims from computer scientists and IT consultants, who purport to offer solutions to technological bottlenecks. In contrast, we draw lessons from a series of recipes for disaster as exemplified in a number of detailed case studies.

As technology cannot be completely reliable, a human-centred approach to management of information technology in organisations is presented, with practical guidance on how to proceed. As all managers find themselves users of IT, it is no longer sensible to delegate all responsibility to others: all managers have become managers of information technology, and must face up to the prospects and challenges of IT disasters.

Theory is fine, but there is no substitute for experience. This book is intended to help the reader to benefit from the experience of others, and to question the practice of his or her organisation in a way that makes IT disasters less likely.

At Kingston Business School we have benefited from the support of a skilled technical support team, led by Colin Butler with network management from Ted Slade, in close association with John Bird and Brenda Ness of the University Computing Service. Their skill has sustained the environment in which this work has been conducted, and they have contributed greatly to the author's understanding of the practical realities of system management and disaster prevention. I am grateful for the advice and support of the series co-editor, Phil Molyneux of Kingston Business School, and the Publishing Director, John Watson, of Springer-Verlag London Limited.

Kingston, February 1995   R.E.

Introduction

An information technology disaster is defined as any incident that impairs the effective working of the data-processing function. Given the distribution of data-processing capabilities from central Computing Departments to managers across organisations, disasters can also be distributed in their pattern of occurrence and in their impacts.

All staff can be affected by IT disasters. Many have the power to cause disasters, of different scales. Few understand the different dependences that parts of the organisation have on IT for their operation and survival.

For many organisations, IT disasters only exist once discovered. Until that stage, IT operations may be problematic but have no visible adverse impact. Indeed, it may be considered advisable, from the perspective of corporate image, to act as if IT disasters do not take place. Crisis management can be seen as a public-relations issue.

The activity of suppressing consideration of systems failures and problems can be dangerous. It may mean that the safety valve, necessary for safe operation of systems, is removed. When the disaster becomes unavoidably apparent, it may be too late for countermeasures.

There is a tendency for companies to seek to disguise developing disasters, until it is too late. In-house approaches will be used rather than bringing in external consultants, who could pose a threat to the organisation's self-image. Alternatively, consultants may be called in as a substitute for local consideration of sensitive issues.

In areas where official secrecy is involved, the existence of a problem will itself be an official secret. High security clearance is required, and the capacity to consult users is impaired, unless this is done indirectly. On the other hand, the implementation of security measures may lead to a false confidence among those who lack understanding of the nature and potential of IT disasters.

Disasters: Some Examples

Beautiful Railway Bridge of the Silv'ry Tay!
Alas, I am very sorry to say
That ninety lives have been taken away
On the last Sabbath day of 1879,
Which will be remember'd for a very long time.

William McGonagall (1825–1902), The Tay Bridge Disaster

Information technology and software engineering may be thought to be almost as well formed as McGonagall's poetry. All too frequently they are the product of the well-meaning but untrained enthusiast. Information technology has been sold as providing all the solutions. In practice, it can lead to disasters that had not previously been considered.

WAITING TO HAPPEN

Hard Luck

A new secretary deletes the contents of a hard disk, losing all the data that had not been backed up. As the system lacked user documentation, she did not know what to do, or whom to ask. Her manager had previously left such technical details to her predecessor, and did not use the technology himself. No initial training was provided. After all, the system was sold as being "user-friendly".

Hard Feelings

A disgruntled sacked employee leaves a "time-bomb" on the company computer system, wiping out all files on a preset date or diverting funds to an external account. He was not employed as a Systems Engineer, but used his access to the company network to gain entry to key files, evading detection. This phenomenon explains the growing practice of immediate removal of technically competent staff at the time of dismissal.

Rebuilding Societies

Two Building Societies seek to merge, but their senior managers have to face the complications of incompatible computer systems. It takes some months before it is agreed that systems incompatibilities cannot be resolved, and talks are abandoned. It is suggested that incompatible systems may have been installed as a means of preventing take-over: a form of poison pill. IT was central to both success and failure in mergers and acquisitions. With the additional complication of regulatory systems, this problem may increase.

Outsourcing

A high-technology manufacturing company contracts out the work of its IT Department to a systems integration consultancy; it loses control of what is regarded as a key competitive weapon. The consultancy works in close association with hardware vendors who have been the company's competitors on previous competitive bids. Questions are asked about confidentiality, independence and information flows. As the company divests itself of non-core subsidiaries, it may be thought to have lost control over its own strategic direction. Financial engineering may not be sufficient.

Out of Windows

A company declares "Windows" to be the company standard environment, while many employees have computers with insufficient power. Communications across the company break down until major investments in upgrading are made, together with company-wide training. Discontinuities in communication and applications use can prove expensive. Upgrades do not always meet the promised specifications. Individual enthusiasts may have to be restrained.

Taking Stock

The Stock Exchange TAURUS computer system was abandoned after many years and considerable expense of development work. London is in danger of losing its competitive advantage as a high-technology business centre, and the credibility of technical systems in financial institutions is imperilled. The Lloyds Insurance market, devoid of coordinating technology, and discredited following years of losses, compounds the disaster for City institutions. City professions may need complete overhaul.

Insiders

Transaction monitoring systems have not been installed by regulatory bodies to support enforcement of Financial Services legislation. Dealers engaged in insider trading are enabled to continue unchecked, and the system of compliance falls into increasing disrepute. Lack of IT in strategic situations can constitute a disaster. Regulations became, like tax, something to be avoided, or evaded.

Shrinking Blue

IBM gave effective control of its personal-computer operating systems to Microsoft. Whereas IBM had in the past developed operating systems using in-house teams, on this occasion an external contract was given, without control being retained by IBM, resulting in Microsoft growing to exceed the capitalisation of IBM. IBM had led the development of the industry, and has been reduced to the status of a follower. The epitome of the IT industry has experienced a disastrous change. Senior managers in other companies may be making similar mistakes, without understanding the dangers.

Hacking by Appointment

A hacker broke into Prince Philip's Telecom Gold mailbox. This took place during a demonstration programme on live television, emphasising the vulnerability of the technology and the self-proclaiming ethos of hackers.

More dangerous incidents have occurred with the Internet system, as students have gained access to defence computer systems. The Pentagon reports that hackers have been using the Internet to look at new aircraft and ship designs, simulated battle plans, correspondence and even payslips. Information has been stolen or deleted. Military readiness has been impaired.

Internet developed as a tool for the militarily funded academic research community, but is now open to users with a different ethos. Hackers need only install a simple program to snatch every password passing through the system, and store them for later use. More than a million passwords appear to have been stolen. A Highway Code may be required for the information superhighway. If a hacker in country A accesses a database in country B containing personal details relating to residents of countries C and D, who can prosecute the hacker? Whose data-protection laws apply?

Emergency

The London Ambulance Service embarked on the computerisation of their despatch system, overriding the advice of their own professionals and accepting a low tender from a consultancy firm with no previous experience of comparable systems. When the system went "live", without a period of dual working with manual systems, it failed to cope with the scale and complexity of demands, and had to be withdrawn from service. A number of patient deaths have been attributed to the system failure. London Ambulance Service is now bottom of the NHS league tables, with drastic consequences for residents of the capital.

Don't Ask Me

The national railway timetable is being abandoned with the privatisation of British Rail. This national database is a by-product of a national system, and is an unremarked casualty of "reforms". Instead, a junior executive is charged with the responsibility of ensuring that timetable planning of the privatised companies is coordinated, though each declines to make available the timetables of its neighbours and commercial rivals.

There have been losses of analogous national databases in the National Health Service and in Education, as administration has been devolved to self-governing trusts and grant-maintained institutions, each reluctant to share previously public information. One way of avoiding national scrutiny is to remove the national database, and to concentrate instead on "league tables" derived from a careful selection of quantitative performance indicators. For those concerned with access to information on public transport, health or education, these are major IT disasters. IT demonstrates the signs of deeper disasters.

Listening In

All international facsimile transmissions are intercepted by the intelligence services, prejudicing commercial and official secrets. An enhanced version of Internet will include "Clipper" encryption technology. With the ending of the Cold War, it is natural that the intelligence services should undergo their own form of privatisation. Public-domain versions of encryption software are now available via Internet itself, casting doubt on the robustness of many existing security systems. Privacy and freedom-of-information legislation does not exist in the UK, and data-protection legislation makes exceptions for the intelligence services. Inappropriate interception of communications can have disastrous results.

Maintaining Systems

A complex commercial database ceases effective functioning through lack of maintenance. IT services need to be delivered over the long term, with ongoing support costs to be met. Policy changes and corporate restructuring can have disastrous impacts on IT, if databases lack the flexibility to adjust to external circumstances. Where they are adjusted, consistency must be maintained with regard to past and present data. For example, Higher Education institutions need technology to support their decision-making on student admissions and finance, yet the rules and definitions change by the week. Government policies can constitute IT disasters.

New Models

Errors and confusion can arise through transferring data between spreadsheets using different models. Spreadsheet use has become widespread, but understanding is limited. Mistaken use of software tools can result in apparent losses and consequent redundancies: localised IT disasters with lasting impact. A little knowledge can turn out to be a dangerous thing.

Experts and Systems

A skilled worker is replaced by an expert system. Three years later it is realised that the system does not perform some key parts of the job; no human experts are available. The impact on the organisation is disastrous, and the damage to the skill of the professional may be beyond repair. The parts that are lost when an organisation "downsizes" through business process re-engineering and the use of technology may turn out to be vital and irreplaceable.

Closed Shops

Someone is excluded from an effective electronic closed shop by not having access to appropriate technology. Skills that would benefit the organisation are denied, diminishing the quality of decisions. Whole groups can be excluded, identified in terms of disability, geographical location, or occupational group. Systems procurement may be undertaken by managers who do not understand such issues, but are influenced by media reports of new or emerging "industry standards".

Fast and Loose

Software is declared to be in use illegally. Federation Against Software Theft (FAST) rules impose strict licences and policing requirements. Non-standard software may fail to interface with approved hardware and software systems, or have unpredictable side-effects. The use of illegal software may render insurance or maintenance void.

Viral Infection

Viruses may corrupt programs across an organisation. It is unusual that they are developed in-house, but, once they affect company machines, eradication may be difficult and expensive, even disastrous, unless rigorous procedures are in place. A specialist application package, together with large amounts of data, may be installed on the hard disk of a networked computer. Despite virus-checking, a virus is introduced into the system, corrupting the hard disk and necessitating re-formatting. This may in turn require assistance from the original vendors and from consultants.

In Confidence

Confidentiality is threatened by the development of networking. Personal computers have not developed in a culture of security, as have mainframes. The culture change can be disastrous for working practices. Computer-supported cooperative working without a culture of cooperation is unlikely to work. The proliferation of electronic networking is outstripping human networking. It helps to know who is at the other end of the wire!

Out of Service

An organisation develops enhanced networking facilities, with local- and wide-area networking, electronic mail and standard software supported by powerful servers. As part of a spate of burglaries, the key server is stolen while in use. Unless the files have been constantly backed up, electronic correspondence will be lost, and may be beyond reconstruction. It may be months or years before the loss of a short period of electronic traffic becomes known; no answer to an electronic mail message may be construed as the answer "no".

Data Day

Inaccuracies are found in personal-computer data. Perfect accuracy is inconceivable, and monitoring procedures have their practical limits. Inaccurate data can proliferate across systems by means of computations involving central databases, making rectification of errors nearly impossible. As a result, separate divisions of the organisation may prefer to develop their own incompatible systems.

Ignorance and Bliss

Crucial files are kept secret. Access may be on a "need-to-know" basis, based on a past interpretation of who needed to know. Ignorance can prove disastrous. Public Interest Immunity Certificates, brought to public attention in the Scott Inquiry on the sale of arms to Iraq by British companies, are a symbol of a secret society. Network managers may operate a similar culture, protecting their own lack of knowledge.

Uniforms

New software purchased for an organisation may not be compatible with the old. As a wider range of staff are engaged in software purchasing, there is a need for standards and procedures to prevent disastrous and expensive mistakes. Provision of a uniform environment across organisations may mean an unacceptably low level of technology for specialist users.

Betraying Trust

With successive reforms of the National Health Service, responsibility for information systems and security has been devolved to the local level, with each Trust responsible for determining strategy and standards. Overall standards and comparability may be at risk. Information is no longer shared between what have become competitors, each concerned with their own institutional profitability, and the costs of that breakdown of cooperation will be borne by others.

Upgrading

New operating systems and user environments fail to support previous applications. Organisations naturally wish to retain past applications under new software environments, but software developers feel no obligation to maintain upgrade paths if it is not in their commercial interest so to do. Vendors and users work with different, conflicting assumptions: Vendors assume that users will keep paying for licences and upgrades, and that they will conform. Even after a commercial divorce, they expect maintenance payments. Once payments cease, responsibilities are abandoned. Users see no reason to continue maintenance payments, and prefer to replace systems when they cease to meet requirements.

The result is periods of instability and discontinuity, often experienced as IT disasters.

Leakage

Confidential data leak to a commercial rival. Data in the wrong hands can be disastrous. Data are not neutral, but can be a powerful weapon depending on the knowledge and intentions of the user. Disasters are not therefore simply a matter of technology, but of business in the widest sense.

One person's disaster is another's successful strategy. Airlines make use of common booking systems, involving sharing of data. The Virgin customer database fell into the hands of British Airways. In a much-publicised "dirty tricks" campaign, customers were contacted and encouraged to change their travel plans to fly with a competitor. False rumours were spread concerning Virgin's financial position. The IT-based ploy has been turned to the advantage of Virgin, with disastrous outcomes for British Airways, and the senior management team of the day. A crisis for Virgin may have become a disaster for British Airways.

Firing

Unauthorised staff gain access to commercial information. Internal power structures can be disastrously affected by access to information. For example, information about planned redundancies in the hands of the trade unions could prove disruptive of smooth labour relations. Security measures ostensibly to protect data may have the additional purpose of restricting the activities and effectiveness of trade unions. Conversely, trade unions that make full use of new technology may pioneer changes in workplace organisation.

Fatal Advice

An expert system may give advice that leads to the death of a user. As systems are used in areas of tax, environmental regulation and handling of hazardous substances, machines are used where previously human experts would have been involved. Disastrous consequences of computer program operations may be seen as IT disasters, while the software was simply a representation of the expertise of the human expert. There are unresolved questions of responsibility for such disasters, though codes of conduct have been developed by concerned professionals. As IT use becomes widespread, there are issues for the professions, for the law and for democracy itself.

Spare Planet

Testing of critical software can be banned for security reasons. Star Wars is the key example: testing the Strategic Defense Initiative system would have required the use of a spare planet. Actual deployment would therefore have been of an untested system, with potentially disastrous consequences. At the time, issues of security prevented full public discussion; that argument no longer applies. How many other safety-critical systems have not undergone sufficient testing, and will security restrictions mean that we only learn of their existence when they fail?

HUMAN DECISIONS

In each of the cases above, we have to consider human decisions in the context of technology. It is not enough to focus attention on the technology in isolation. Some common practical questions must be asked:

- Who made the decisions?
- Who had the necessary knowledge?
- Who stands to gain?
- Who stands to lose?
- What remedial action can be taken?

In the modern world of business, how can a disaster not involve IT? While the real underlying problems involve people and organisations, it can sometimes be useful to blame the system.

- What do we have to understand to make sense of an IT disaster in a given specialist area?
- What is the role of standards and regulations in a market economy?
- What should be the extent of commercial confidentiality?

This is a new and relatively uncharted area. Technology has been installed on the assumption that it will work according to specification, and it has not been fashionable to consider how to proceed if disaster strikes. This book is a modest attempt to demystify the subject in the hope that improved understanding may help to prevent some disasters.

Disaster Prevention Through Skill

Disasters cannot, with certainty, be prevented, but they can be made less likely, and their impact reduced. The answer lies in human knowledge, both propositional and tacit. To err is human; to really foul things up, use a computer! Powerful tools in the wrong hands can cause considerable damage. Power drills are useful, but it is not sensible to give them to children.

COMPUTATIONAL CONDOMS

Computer viruses have achieved plague proportions during the same years that have seen the spread of AIDS. There is no "computational condom" that can protect the computer user from all possible side-effects. There could be no perfect antivirus protection: even the household disinfectant "Domestos" only guarantees to kill *known* germs, and we could not know that we had identified and protected against viruses and germs as-yet unknown. "Safe sex" offers relative, rather than complete, security, for acts between consenting adults. "Safe computing" needs to encompass use by others, and communication between strangers over considerable distances and across cultural barriers. Certain protocols must be followed, and standards must be observed, in order to minimise the danger of disasters.

"Safe management of computing" requires quality assurance of hardware, software and, above all, people. Networking provides the benefits of rapid communication, but brings with it exposure to risk of precipitate disaster. Security and survival depend on social intercourse without promiscuity.

SUPPRESSION

One answer to reports of impending disaster is suppression. If nobody knows what is going on, discussion and subversion will have less impact, and order can be preserved. On the other hand, publication could provide a safety valve. Whistle-blowers may prevent disaster by precipitating crisis. Lasting security may be strengthened by the provision of channels of dissent, means by which unofficial views can be expressed. The use of inappropriate channels can open up fault lines within organisations.

At the heart of the issue is trust. Can individuals be trusted not to abuse the capacity to publish? If not, what does this say about the autonomy of the professional, and the robustness of modern democracy?

CRISIS MANAGEMENT

Crisis can become disaster in the absence of skill. When a problem arises, individuals need to be capable of responding with appropriate knowledge and experience, and empowered to do so within a supportive and communicative collaborative context. Individuals need to feel ownership of, not alienation from, the processes of production, distribution and exchange of which they form part. Division of labour and the de-skilling of the workforce make organisations more vulnerable to disaster.

Crises place organisations under stress. Where individuals have the strength and flexibility to respond and withstand strain, the organisation may be saved from collapse. Part of the capacity to respond may derive from organisational structures, both formal and informal. Organisations can develop resilience in the face of crisis, which forestalls escalation into disaster.

The individual and organisational dimensions are both tested in times of crisis. Individual decision-making needs to be facilitated by organisational solidarity. If official values are maintained only through lip-service, they are illusory. IT disasters do not occur in isolation, but flow from human decisions in environments that increasingly include IT. We need to understand decisions and decision-making, as well as the potential and limitations of the technology. Disasters are often "waiting to happen", and it would help if we could see this in advance rather than concluding it after the event.

DISASTER RECOVERY

Disaster recovery planning offers new insights into organisations and management, once account is taken of exposure to IT disasters. Recovery planning in itself makes disasters less likely, and may change the working of the organisation. Traditional disaster recovery planning concentrated on physical threats, such as fire, flood and theft. Understanding is now developing of the dangers of defective hardware and software systems, corrupted data and flawed management of information systems. Network communications may bring threats from unseen and unwelcome electronic visitors from anywhere in the world, or beyond.

Disaster recovery planning can highlight weaknesses and dependences, including information flows, reliance on decisions and processing by others, and areas of uncertainty and incomplete information. It enables organisations to use the prospect of disaster as a focus for reflection on management structures and procedures.

IT is playing an increasing role in both disasters and disaster recovery. Where business transactions become complex, IT is seen as a means of making them manageable; when fraud, corruption or disaster strikes, IT is likely to be involved. IT is thus a tool for both the perpetrator and the investigator. IT must be understood by the manager, who will ultimately face the consequences of disaster. If the IT Manager fails to demonstrate understanding to the satisfaction of his superiors, he may find that he has become superfluous and the management of IT has been outsourced.

Fraud: Management in Crisis

COMPLACENCY

The City of London Police have sought to prevent fraud, and published the *Fraudstop* report in 1989. They found that:

> *"The larger the organisation, the easier for it to believe that its internal controls will protect it against fraud. The longer established the organisation, and the more crime-free its experience, the easier for it to believe that it is immune from serious attack by fraud."* (p. 1)

Faced with a prevailing mood of complacency, they argue the case for action:

> *"Nobody enjoys contemplating the circumstances and effects of his own demise, and yet it is a foolish man who does not spend sufficient time in such a pursuit as to make a Will so that if the unexpected happens, there will be no doubt in the minds of others as to his intentions, and there will be a plan of action for others to follow."* (p. 1)

It is perhaps unsurprising that they found an emphasis on financial controls, rather than insights into areas of technical exposure:

> *"The extent of the average City company's fraud policy and planning appears to be confined to the design, installation and supervision of efficient financial control systems."* (p. 11)

CHANGE

There is a mismatch between conventional approaches to management and management education, and the environment of constant change in which managers now have to work. Many of the traditional supports and resources have been removed, timescales have been concentrated, and restructuring around processes and projects implies navigation through unfamiliar waters.

Management gurus have been shown to have feet of clay. The award of the title "*Guardian* Young Businessman of the Year" can prove terminal to the career of the manager in question. John Harvey-Jones has been trouble-shooter for others, but has run into troubles of his own in his recent board positions.

Charles Handy, extraordinarily perceptive about the directions of organisational change, has accepted, in his *The Empty Raincoat* [Handy 1994], that the changes have been painful for many of the people involved:

> *"Capitalism has not proved as flexible as it was supposed to be. Governments have not been all-wise or far-seeing. Life is a struggle for many and a puzzle for most."*

> *"The more we know, the more confused we get; ... the more we increase our technical capacity the more powerless we become."*

The new focus on process reinforces the need for managers to have experience and understanding of the areas in which they have direct management responsibilities. Practice, and reflection on practice, becomes critical. The concept of general management is under challenge, at least in the conventional sense. Middle managers are an endangered species, and their career expectations have changed. The kind of organisation for which they had prepared has ceased to exist. New skills are required.

CRISES

Between crisis management and disaster recovery lies the key ground.

- How can crisis be prevented from becoming disaster?
- Can disaster recovery planning itself form part of the answer?
- Should a company be organised around the processes that are critical for its survival?

We are concerned to prevent IT disasters, but this requires understanding of complex issues. We need to:

- Accept the limitations of our knowledge, preparing the way to learn from the knowledge and experience of others.
- Identify those whose roles and expertise are critical if and when disaster strikes: they may not be accorded appropriate recognition during the smooth running times of the organisation.
- Understand the organisational changes that may be facilitated by IT and that may help to forestall disaster: this can be termed "business process re-engineering".

When IT systems go down, the future of the organisation may depend on rapid recovery. This, in turn, depends on the knowledge of specialists, who need to be available and committed. All too often the value of technical knowledge is under-appreciated, in status and financial terms. Rewards are given to those more closely linked with attributable financial returns, who may work in finance or marketing.

The answer may lie in ownership. If the technical specialist feels ownership of the system she is developing and supporting, she will offer instinctive commitment in times of trouble. If she is merely contracted to work for a defined number of hours on a system belonging to others, the relationship is different. There is also an issue of parity of esteem. When there is a crisis, communication needs to be open if a disaster is to be averted. Open communication requires a backdrop of trust, developed and tested over time.

The attitude of users is critical if crisis is not to develop into disaster. Once users see technical support staff as "them", and not as colleagues of equivalent status, they can find it acceptable to slough off responsibility, requiring the technical support team to have technical knowledge they themselves lack.

CHOICES

Once the system is seen in human terms, the pivotal and weak links emerge as human rather than technological. Machines can neither understand nor misunderstand, but can operate in channels established through human agency. Choices surface in financial terms. Limited resources will have to cover both collective security and individual processing power, and organisations will have to withstand the pressures from those denied the desired facilities. Overall capabilities may be perceived as declining while expectations rise.

Timescales matter. A long-term perspective is required for investments in infrastructure, communications and security. It will be cheaper in the short term to skimp, to cut costs, or to contract the service out. Organisations who take this approach may not exist in the longer term.

Contracting out the strategic and operational management of IT is tantamount to irreversibly abdicating key strategic management functions, restricting future choices. To the extent that IT is regarded as integral to corporate strategy, this may be a serious or fatal mistake.

Lessons can be learned from cases of IT disasters.

THE BISHOPSGATE BOMB

At 10.30 on the morning of Saturday 24th April 1993, a 3 tonne bomb exploded in Bishopsgate in the City of London, causing enormous damage to more than two-million square feet of office space across 40 acres. The IRA claimed responsibility.

A total of 750 businesses in one of the world's busiest financial centres were affected by the blast. The Long Term Credit Bank of Japan, located at 55 Bishopsgate, took the full force of the explosion. The damage to the building and equipment was substantial. Staff faced the onerous task of bringing the bank back to business as soon as possible.

The bank had long realised the need for contingency planning and had well established business recovery procedures in place. Reliant on IT systems to conduct all financial transactions, they had taken the precaution of drawing up an IT recovery contract with IBM.

Lessons for Major Corporations

Bishopsgate was a disaster on a grand scale that received a great deal of media attention. It highlighted the fact that arson, sabotage, flooding and even denial of access in the aftermath of terrorist activity can bring a business to its knees. Different areas of risk need to be considered as a matter of urgency.

Denial of access was a major factor affecting businesses following the Bishopsgate bomb. Even where offices were intact, the police exclusion zone, which covered a half-mile radius, meant that some staff were not allowed into their offices for 48 hours, and if staff cannot get to their telephones and computers, their customers cannot reach them. The short-term impact on the business can be just as significant as suffering physical bomb damage.

Disaster Strikes

There are also more mundane disasters, such as hardware failure, power failure and human error to be considered. Statistics abound on the impact to business performance: one financial institution wrote off £2 million after a 2 hour power failure, while the average computer fire costs £3.7 million.

Business protection is not just a commercial matter, but a legal one: under the Data Protection and Computer Misuse Acts, companies are obliged to safeguard the information they hold. Yet at the time of Bishopsgate, many businesses did not have plans in place to deal with the recovery of their business. The law was not seen as a priority concern.

A report published just days before the Bishopsgate bomb found that one in five organisations suffer a major disaster to their computing facilities, yet four out of five UK organisations did not have a viable contingency plan. This means that, if disaster struck, 78% of businesses would not be able to cope.

The research conducted by Loughborough University concluded that even those organisations with contingency plans may find themselves woefully unprepared. This is because their plans do not include recovery of the business as well as the computer system, or else have not been tested within the last six months. Unless tested, a plan is just a list of theoretically good ideas. The research found that in the financial services industry, critically affected by Bishopsgate and heavily dependent on computer systems, only 44% actually had a viable plan in operation.

Chief Inspector Moore of the Metropolitan Police is responsible for strategy and implementation of anti-terrorist campaigns in the City.

"It still surprises me that some companies do not have any plans to deal with disasters. This bombing has to be set against a much bigger background. There are

currently some 100 active terrorist organisations, any of which could carry out similar disruptive activities."

He was also concerned in light of the fact that even those people with contingency plans were coming up to exclusion cordons at the scene of the Bishopsgate bomb to ask if they could retrieve recovery plans for their building.

"We cannot allow people to access their building after a disaster like that. It's obviously a major investigation scene and companies won't be allowed back until we have finished."

Preventive Medicine

The Bishopsgate bomb demonstrated that lightning can strike twice: some companies hit by the St Mary's Axe bomb in April 1992 were struck again in 1993. Operations were forced to seriously consider the implications of disaster and examine the implementation of contingency planning for business recovery.

For a long time disaster recovery merely meant backing up the computer disk, but in a real disaster, everything from the office premises to the scribbled Post-it note with the latest new business leads is at risk. It is pointless recovering IT systems if the rest of the business is still not up and running to deal with customers. Business recovery planning should cover all aspects of the business: from the loss of the building to the loss of stationery, from dealing with media attention to helping staff.

Some of the largest companies provide their own complete back-up systems, including alternative office space. But for the majority, this simply isn't cost-effective, and since Bishopsgate many are looking to specialist companies to provide them with a recovery service.

From this case we can conclude that there are several areas of disaster recovery planning that companies cannot afford to neglect:

- Implement a clean-desk policy.
- Think of business, not just IT, recovery.
- A plan is only a list of good ideas unless tested.
- Potential denial of access should not be overlooked.
- Recovery plans, vital records and data must be stored off-site.
- Recovery plans should include crisis management.
- Control centres must be predetermined.
- Fall-back options with a European link need to be considered.
- Insurance cover alone is not adequate protection.
- Reciprocal arrangements are not viable.

One Year On

A year after Bishopsgate, businesses were taking the threat of disaster very seriously. Many began to take a critical look at existing plans, or worked to introduce contingency planning. Some, of course, are no longer trading.

The City of London has also stepped up its defences against future terrorist attacks with a new emergency service. The City of London Emergency Help Desk will give year-round, 24 hour a day emergency cover to help businesses in the event of disaster. While it is certainly not a substitute for every organisation preparing its own business recovery plan, a number of companies will provide specialist advice on every aspect of business recovery if the City suffers a major incident.

For their part, the police have restricted vehicle access to the square mile. There are just eight entry points, each manned 24 hours a day. Vehicle registrations are logged, and photos of occupants are taken. The City of London Police has also launched a Camera Watch closed-circuit television scheme for the continuous monitoring of the area, and is examining a pager alert system.

It is hard to see how resources could be found for similar measures in other areas. The measures may be seen as little more than symbolic.

CORPORATE SECURITY AND DISASTER PREVENTION

As technology progresses, as our computer networks grow and as our means of communication become more and more complex, corporate secrets become less and less secure.

Espionage

- British Airways are in the process of recovering their losses and mending their reputation after media coverage of their attempt to poach customers from their competitor, Virgin Airlines.
- For Europarks, the car-park giant who recently found vast amounts of information regarding their finances in the hands of their competitors NCP, industrial espionage was by no means a creation of the media.
- The ongoing feud between General Motors and Volkswagen, where a senior manager was accused of taking plans with him when he moved, contains the classic elements of a spy novel.
- In 1991, the former Head of French Intelligence, Pierre Marion, revealed that first-class Air France passengers were being bugged on transatlantic flights, and that their briefcases were opened and searched while they slept in order to find information that would be useful to French companies.

The gleaning of information is often so easy that an outside investigation company is not needed. Within the area of telecommunications, the ease with which someone can monitor and intercept private conversation is remarkable. It does not require much technical know-how to simulate an input device capable of diverting messages to another location. Nor are the other telecommunications systems totally secure: fax and telex are just as easily bugged. Since the ending of the Cold War, the expertise of intelligence agents has been turned to commercial ends. The transition from agent to management consultant has been smooth!

Security of Assets

In many British businesses, the security of assets is often overlooked. No company today would try to run its business without the help of a computer, yet as little as 15% of users protect against the loss of these machines and, more importantly, the data on them.

A power failure wreaked havoc in the offices of *The Independent* newspaper shortly after its launch. The staff found themselves producing the paper by hand under the light of a candle. Since then the company has installed a sophisticated uninterruptable power supply (UPS).

A spokesman for Procurement Services, a company involved in protecting companies against terrorist attacks, claims that 15 damaging attacks take place in the UK each day. The victims often find it commercially preferable to restrict publicity.

The Computer Security Industry

As a response to growing dependence on the company mainframe, the computer security industry was born in the USA in the late 1970s. It was then a question of guarding the data-storage machine, monitoring the temperature and humidity of the computer room and protecting an investment, and it was a small industry. By the late 1980s, many of the major players in the IT industry were involved in advising and implementing strategies for clients concerned about loopholes in their businesses' electronic information culture.

Today IT disasters are a multi-million-pound business. Proof of success is when nothing happens, or when nothing is reported as having happened. The security practitioners are constantly struggling to stay ahead of the game. The 1993 Code of Practice for security, produced by the DTI, is soon to become a BSI standard, and inevitably a key business insurance issue. Who should be trusted to implement such standards?

The evolution of IT security issues into this sophisticated and expanding industry is mirrored in the shift of responsibility for these things from the Systems Manager to the Company Chairman. The discussion is now carried out in the Boardroom, where Directors are being made to realise their dependence on the IT infrastructure, and the precariousness of the day-to-day operations that they take for granted. The core activities of a company must be identified by a risk analysis, so that the cornerstone of "business continuity" can be depended upon even after a natural disaster or terrorist attack. Many Directors and Managers may turn out to be superfluous to the delivery of that core.

One area ignored by a company at their peril is the cashflow procedure of the customer-services operation. Some 70% of businesses go under within

18 months of a crisis, and unless the influx of funds is protected, the initial disaster will undoubtedly prove to be the death-blow. While financial institutions such as banks take a short-term approach to lending and investment, companies may find themselves on their own in case of disaster.

Hackers

Hackers alone are not responsible for the estimated £1.1 billion lost every year through security breaches. The 1990 Computer Misuse Act has assured that the hacker, when caught, can face serious charges. An alternative outcome is employment of the hacker by the organisation whose system has been penetrated.

Many experts believe that the internal threat is greater than that of the outside hacker. As a result of downsizing from the central control of data to distribution over local- or wide-area networks, information is now increasingly open to abuse by the rapidly changing workforce because of the increase in access methods. You can choose to protect the PC network with software that blocks the use of functions not held on a list of authorised programs. Encryption of data by hardware or software is the most widely implemented solution, in which confidential information is made readable (decrypted) only after the user has been identified as friend rather than foe. This assumes that the encryption software is itself immune to hacking – a questionable assumption.

The CBI emphasises that security procedures are not enough. It is important to consider the structures of communication and management as factors in an effective risk analysis. Motivation for wilful corruption of data, or the introduction of a software virus, is often the same as for financial fraud against employers: a sense of dissatisfaction and resentment. A secure environment needs to be created by a positive atmosphere and example from the top as well as by steel safes for file servers.

Back-Up Sites

An unanswered phone is a common business occurrence, but one that continues to ring in the headquarters of a major bank can result in its total collapse. Few organisations will emerge unscathed from a full communications collapse. A power failure in Wall Street in 1990 cost related business $100 million. In 1993 the Bishopsgate bomb left Natwest unoperational for several days.

Back-up sites span a range of options, costs and degrees of comfort. In some important applications, where a disruption in business would be very costly, companies have a fully operational mirrored office, replete with identical network. Fibre optics can allow the computer systems at both the original and back-up sites to be identical at all times. This is unusual. Most companies will arrange for data to be sent down to the site at regular intervals, or alternatively to be sent down over more secure dedicated ISDN links in the event of a disaster.

In most cases, a company can be up and running to full capacity within hours of breakdown or attack. ACT Financial Services have set up a back-up site

15 minutes away from the City, drawing on a different power supply. The close proximity of the site means that, in the event of a close-down, computers could be up and running within minutes, depending, of course, on how fast the employees can run. An American-based recovery service has developed a mobile work area recovery centre, which is delivered to the site and assembled within 48 hours.

The question is then about the ability of the staff of the organisation to maintain critical functions despite and during the relocation of IT facilities. Would they be wiser to rely on back-up sites for the management of their IT facilities on a regular basis, passing on the apparent risks and challenges of dealing with IT disasters?

Or, alternatively, is there an approach to disaster prevention that does not involve abdicating and outsourcing?

Systems and Decision-Making

I must Create a System, or be enslav'd by another Man's;
I will not Reason and Compare: my business is to Create.

William Blake (1757–1827), Jerusalem

Behind the recent flurry of activity provoked by well publicised IT disasters, there are deeper and more fundamental concerns.

DEPENDENCE ON SYSTEMS

There are dangers in dependence on systems. This applies to real-time systems operating without human intervention, but also to methods and methodologies that take no account of changing circumstances and cultural differences. Information systems represent reifications of ideologies. On the other hand, large organisations need to develop common procedures to be followed by all, inhibiting individual freedom of choice.

Companies, and individual managers, may fail to understand the limits of their systems and technology. They may come to believe their own advertising communications, written without technical understanding. We cannot put forward a foolproof system for preventing IT disasters, as our thesis is that dependence on systems is in itself a major cause of disasters, and the only reliable approach to prevention is the empowerment of human decision-making and communication.

Where computers have taken on tasks previously performed by humans, the skills required to perform the tasks may fade and vanish. Disasters may flow from past decisions, and from ongoing management approaches, whose consequences and interactions may be hard or impossible to predict.

INFORMATION TECHNOLGY ON THE MARGINS

IT use may be divorced from IT decision-making. There is a tendency for senior managers to delegate responsibility for IT and its management to subordinates, although IT decisions may be fundamental to the future of the organisation. IT strategy may be integrated with the overall thrust of corporate strategy, and yet not understood by strategic decision-makers. IT may have achieved commodity status, but the radical transforming potential is little understood.

An IT disaster is likely to be indicative of broader problems in the organisation. It may be easier to focus on the IT aspect than on division and incoherence at Board level, or false economies implemented by the Finance Director in the name of cost-cutting and efficiency. Ill-considered changes in IT may compound the underlying and untreated malaise.

DEPENDENCE ON VENDORS

Companies may develop a dangerous dependence on vendors, whose advice may distort company strategy and development. There is a case for maintaining an in-house capability to avoid being at the mercy of the unscrupulous salesman, always willing to sell the most expensive system. There is a current vogue for vendors to masquerade as systems integrators or management consultants. Not all clients are fooled.

CSC are a highly successful American-based consultancy, who are expanding their operations in Europe. They see information technology as critical for future competitive advantage, and offer to manage IT operations for major clients, as a systems integrator and outsourcing specialist. They have taken over expensive hotels to stage seminars free of charge for data-processing managers, and to present a clear sales message. Their 1991 Annual Review declared:

"In the 1990s, successful organisations will be those that use information technology imaginatively to competitive advantage. Powerful new technologies enable managers to rethink business strategies, creating new ways of doing business. They enable companies to operate with completely different economies and offerings from those of the past."

BUSINESS RE-ENGINEERING

Consultancies such as CSC argue that new information technologies make the re-engineering of business around key processes possible. Furthermore, the availability of the same technology to competitors makes re-engineering essential. James Champy, chairman of CSC-Index, was co-author, with Michael Hammer, of the best-selling *Reengineering the Corporation: A Manifesto for Business Revolution* [Hammer and Champy 1994]. Among the revolutionary implications of the book is an explosion in IT management consultancy, the modern-day equivalent of Norland's Nannies. Small or worried companies know that Nanny knows best. Business re-engineering has become big business for CSC, where they trade on the complexity of IT:

> *"The daunting complexity of multiple converging technologies can frustrate any organisation trying to go it alone. Information does much more than report on business activities: it changes the very nature of the business itself. In information systems development, results alter the business problem. In this world of non-linear causality, partnership between technology provider and information consumer is essential: together they continually achieve results and change the problem."*

CSC suggest that companies have lost control of their IT functions:

> *"After 30 years of automating and re-automating their business processes, there is little coherent architecture left in the information infrastructure of most large enterprises. Rather there is the almost unmanageable complexity of so many inter-linked systems developed at different times with different technologies."*

Here they identify an opening for a new set of specialists, such as themselves:

> *"The information challenges of the next decade are to re-engineer those business processes for simplicity, to install 90s technology supporting those improved processes, and to migrate the operations of the enterprise smoothly from the old system to the new. These challenges require partnership among business people, re-engineering specialists, information architects, systems developers and change management professionals."*

CAUTION ON CONSULTANCY

The unifying assumption behind competing systems integration companies is that they have the capacity to deliver solutions, and that user organisations should be prepared to pay the premium fees.

Systems integrators tend to focus, not on support for business processes, but on targeting particular vertical markets. As systems integrators achieve their objective of controlling outsourcing of IT services, they will find themselves responsible for the IT support of operations with which they are not familiar, and which are not their central concern. Issues of responsibility and account-ability, not much discussed in IT circles, come to the fore. If IT is the enabling tool for business success and survival, how should we regard those who sell-on the hardware and packages to almost captive clients? Is it significant that many have gained the bulk of their previous experience in the defence and arms markets?

Consultancies may offer formulaic advice, rather than taking account of the particular needs of an individual client. Companies need to be able to evaluate the advice of external consultants, taking the trouble to form hypotheses for discussion. It would be useful to assess the practical experience of those who seek payment for advising on the problems of others.

Once a disaster has occurred, consultants can normally offer a detailed explanation, with recommendations for management. Disasters and insolvencies provide a steady flow of income for consultancies in troubled times, but they have to try to steer clear of cases where their own firms may have been involved. Retrospective auditing is easier than management decision-making, offers more scope for creativity, and tends to be more financially lucrative.

Strategic Functions

HUMAN RESOURCE DEVELOPMENT

Human resource development often fails to take account of IT. Managers and employees must be able to adapt to changing circumstances, which in turn requires a robust basis of education and training, including competence in the use of IT. Given that technology is often introduced as a means of lowering employee head-count, attitudes to new technology and its deployment can be strained.

When things go wrong, you find out who your friends are, and what your own organisation is really about. It is easy enough to cope during years of expansion and profitability: faced with a choice between A and B, there is likely to be a way of choosing both A and B. In a downturn, or when collective morale and finances are faltering, new approaches are needed. The easiest answer is to look the other way, pretending there is no problem. That way, preparations are not made in advance of disaster, which is by definition unexpected, though explicable in retrospect.

On this argument, disasters are likely to proliferate once they start. The danger is that they escalate out of control. One strip of Sellotape may work to hold together one damaged item, but layers of Sellotape become progressively weaker, and give way, making repair and reconstruction necessary.

If people want to bridge gaps, this can reopen possibilities of recovery. Organisations turn out to be made up of people, who choose to exercise judgement and skill rather than simply obeying orders.

The traditional Taylorist approach to management of people [Taylor 1911] is to develop tightly specified job descriptions, limiting the reliance of the organisation on the unreliable human element. At a time of rapid industrial, technological and organisational change, the reverse approach is required. The key resource of the organisation is the workforce, and a full appreciation is required of their individual and collective skills in order to take maximum advantage of the limited capabilities of IT in such contexts. Accompanying this is a necessity for constant staff development.

Security consultants such as EDS, with long experience in defence contracting, emphasise the importance of trusting important IT systems. This is to misunderstand the nature (and grammar) of trust. Trust is a two-way process, which develops through experience over time. It involves an understanding of both strengths and weaknesses. It cannot simply be certified by a purportedly independent external consultancy. Trust is also relative to the conditions in which a relationship obtains, and cannot naively be extrapolated to new, often hypothetical, circumstances. It is hard to trust a commercial company who masquerade as an independent evaluation facility, and have already secured the IT outsourcing contract for the Inland Revenue.

RESEARCH AND DEVELOPMENT

The company may neglect research and development activity that would enable it to keep abreast of IT developments. It is not possible to lead in the development of a particular generation of technology without being actively involved in the use of the previous generation. The Japanese approach of emulating and copying the innovations of overseas rivals, as traditionally practised in the martial arts, has resulted in world leads in the next generation. This was made explicit in the detailed publications of ICOT, the Japanese Fifth Generation Computing Research Institute, as part of the twelfth in a series of major collaborative programmes supported by industry and the Japanese Government. Research and development activity cannot be assured of success, so may carry with it the risk of disaster. The alternative, however, is to stand still and refrain from involvement in the culture of the next generation of technology, from which innovation will spring. Companies will not succeed unless they are prepared to fail, and to learn from their failures. To demand success first time, every time, is self-defeating.

COMPANY COMMUNICATIONS

Company communication structures may not be consistent with communication and networking facilitated by IT. A traditional top-down management structure, with several layers of middle management, will sit uncomfortably with distributed processing and horizontal communication.

Problems can be prevented from becoming disasters by maintaining good communications within a skilled workforce in an open organisation. An organisation divided by class, function and status may not survive disasters. People need to feel that communication will be followed by action, within the context of shared objectives.

Secrecy can be a major cause of IT disasters. Where freedom of information and critical comment is curtailed, purportedly for security purposes against an external threat, internal security is weakened. When an individual detects problems, he may be prevented from taking appropriate remedial action. Secure systems may carry within them the means of their own undoing: it may not be permissible to discuss or deal with problems, and the official policy may be to continue as if all was well. Secrecy impairs the quality of dialogue, as it restricts the freedom of question, answer and explanation.

With the spread of IT, and its use across organisations in all sectors, new groups of professionals find themselves supposedly in control of a technology that has had a specialist language and conceptual structure of its own. Business professionals have typically not had a formal grounding in IT, but use it to articulate the concerns of their own specialist disciplines, such as marketing, finance and human resource management. As such specialist professionals gain in confidence, their expectations and requirements of IT can rise beyond the level where support can be provided. They can give a clearer account of what they want, and dismiss any problems as technical details with which they are not concerned.

HYBRID MANAGERS

Who is to take responsibility for the problem areas where professional require-ments meet technical possibility? This is the area where the hybrid is particularly valuable, with the bilingual capability to speak as both functional professional and technical adviser. In the 1980s the idea of hybrid managers was attractive to the CBI and British Computer Society, who identified a need for many thousands of people experienced and qualified in both management and IT. A flurry of reports was followed by deepening recession, and redundancies for hybrid managers.

It does not follow that implementation and management can be the ongoing responsibility of the hybrid, or we find yet another level of breakdown of communication:

problem domain
↓
specialist professional
↓
hybrid
↓
technical support
↓
technology

The responsibility needs to be shared and jointly owned, if the organisation is to learn from the technical challenges.

An alternative is to resort to outsourcing of all technical support, succumbing to the arguments of management consultants that these ideas are too difficult for non-specialists to manage, and that it is strategically wiser to rely on experienced outsiders. Those who specialise in outsourcing, and in the systems integration, business process re-engineering and channels work that typically precedes it, have developed a charging methodology that takes advantage of client companies at their points of maximum vulnerability, starting with modest charges but ramping up the fees once the balance of power has been changed.

Technical Issues

Each venture
Is a new beginning, a raid on the inarticulate
With shabby equipment always deteriorating
In the general mess of imprecision of feeling.

T. S. Eliot (1888–1965), East Coker

It is fashionable for managers to disregard technical details, focusing on business imperatives. Improved performance and quality will be required, but unfortunately funds are not available for investment in IT infrastructure and facilities. Just when IT was supposed to be user-friendly and available as a commodity, things fall apart.

INTERFACES

Users of powerful systems may be impressed by the user interface but fail to understand the underlying system, and the model that it embodies of the problem to be solved. The spread of graphical user interfaces, such as windowing systems, compounds the problem. The mouse is presented as being natural and intuitive, but its use constitutes programming and requires insight. Speech-driven systems are now available, but require extensive case-study work if we are to learn beneficial applications. Not all secretaries want to be isolated in sound-proof cubicles.

DIFFERING MODELS

Users may assume compatibility between apparently similar systems, but fail to take account of differences in underlying mathematical models. This applies in particular to spreadsheets. Personal-computer spreadsheets such as Visicalc and Lotus 1-2-3 gained enormous sales, and now integrated systems and local-area networks are sold as offering the solution to complex business problems. Little is said of the fact that users are assumed to share an unspecified common model and common language, even if they are using different proprietary packages. It is apparent from the experience of selling non-standard spreadsheets such as Lotus Improv that people find it hard to shed habits acquired with previous generations of computer systems, and that the potential for disasters through misunderstanding is considerable.

MAINTENANCE

Companies may give insufficient attention to maintenance of systems following installation. Hardware and software development costs are as nothing to maintenance costs of installed systems, yet few companies budget for ongoing maintenance, seeing it as a cost to be cut. Maintenance costs soon outstrip the initial costs of purchase of hardware and software.

Applications packages are written in programming environments using computer languages and development tools in an operating system running on a particular hardware configuration. Over time, each of these levels can undergo change, with no necessary obligation felt to provide upgrades and ongoing support. Users may be on their own, and obliged to transfer vast masses of data to new applications in order to stay in business. Unless this is seen as part of support and maintenance, basic organisational functions may be at risk of collapse. Only lawyers benefit from the turmoil that follows, as those involved seek to attribute blame.

DOCUMENTATION

Documentation may be missing, incomplete or misleading. Typically, it will have been left until last by the technically oriented system developer, and not written with the users of the system in mind. Developers rarely use the tools they produce, and may have little insight into the needs and culture of eventual users. User involvement and participation has been the exception rather than the rule, and documentation may not have been subjected to user testing.

LAW

Ignorance of the law can lead to disaster. The law typically moves slowly, but applies to the fast-moving world of IT. Issues include copyright, licensing, data protection, privacy, health and safety, and employment protection. Through their use of IT, companies may be subject to the provisions of national,

European and United States law, as well as to international bodies such as GATT and the ILO. For companies with a high degree of dependence on IT, problems with the law can prove fatal. Innocent third parties may be affected by legal judgements on, for example, spreadsheets with a Lotus-style ("look and feel") interface on sale by rival software houses.

It is argued, particularly by lawyers, that "A man who is his own lawyer has a fool for his client", but this does not mean that all legal issues can be disregarded or left to external legal advisers.

Organisational Cultural Issues

No man is an island, entire of itself; every man is a peice of the Continent, a part of the main; if a clod be washed away by the sea, Europe is the less, as well as if a promontory were, as well as if a manor of the friends or of thine own were; any man's death diminishes me, because I am involved in Mankind; And therefore never send to know for whom the bell tolls; It tolls for thee.

John Donne (?1572–1631), Meditation XVII

The personal computer is no longer a symbol of independence, but one of interdependence. Networks built by radical non-conformists are now obliging users to conform in order to communicate. Successful conformity, however, may require an understanding of dissidence. The Flower Children of the 1960s are running the corporations of the 1990s.

Who needs to be concerned about network management and IT disasters? In today's organisation, nobody is unaffected by a disaster, and the misfortune of one can impact on all.

RESPONSIBILITY

It is substantially a question of responsibility. We may delegate a task to a computer system, but responsibility must remain in human hands. If effective power has passed to the system, then responsibility is negated, and the system is out of control. This in itself may be seen as constituting an IT disaster.

OPEN ORGANISATIONS

Modern organisations aspire to being open systems, with ease of communication, involving all. "Open Systems" was to be the answer to problems of incompatibility, highlighted in mergers between organisations with different data-processing systems and traditions. It has not proved so easy to shake off past traditions in seeking to meet the needs of a new generation of users. As always, some systems are more open than others. George Orwell may be seen as writing about operating systems as well as political systems in his *1984* and *Animal Farm*.

DEALING WITH MODELS

It must be understood that computers cannot deal with reality, but only with models. Even computer systems operating in real time do so with respect to pre-programmed models governing their interpretation of data.

It may be argued that this difficulty is overcome by machine learning and neural networks, but, although we may observe improved performance of such systems over time, the automated agents cannot explain their decisions and behaviour in a manner comprehensible to human agents. We choose whether or not to use such systems, and how much reliance we should place on them: the responsibility for decisions remains ours. Neural networks continue to be black boxes, to which responsibility cannot be ascribed.

COLONIAL EXPERIENCE

It may be that imperial and colonial experience has predisposed the British to prevention of IT disasters. The art of administering a vast Empire was to retain central power but to delegate responsibility, while maintaining reliable reporting lines. The model that applied to colonies world-wide is now being applied to the administration of "market forces", whereby suppliers and consumers are separated and distinguished, and competition is stimulated. Previously, public education and health services have been national, and nationally accountable: dissent is stifled through fragmentation, possibly preventing political disaster for Government.

ROLE CONFUSION

Role confusion can be more general. When different models of management are yoked together and supported by IT systems, problems and disasters may arise at the interstices, amplified by role confusion experienced by agents and organisations. There are particular problems for consultants, who may act as objective advisers, competing contractors and professional auditors, possibly with all roles running in parallel with divisions of the organisation in theory separated by "Chinese Walls". Examples include Wessex Health Authority, Guinness, BCCI and Carrian.

Intelligent Solutions

KNOWLEDGE-BASED SYSTEMS

Artificial intelligence and knowledge-based systems were presented, particularly by American exponents in search of funding, as the answer to problems of IT in business. In light of a number of technological disasters, confidence has faded, and companies require considerable persuasion to invest in new technology.

It has become fashionable to attack proponents of artificial intelligence as prophets of a false god. Their mission, it is alleged, was to build computer brains. Searle described this as "strong AI". The European approach to AI has been more pragmatic and instrumental: AI tools have enabled us to explore new aspects of problems that challenge our human intelligence.

Commercial knowledge-based systems fall somewhere between these two categories: their ambitions are focused on successful application in particular domains, and they are the product of a process of knowledge engineering. Work with knowledge-based systems has provided us with new insights into skill and technology. It was assumed in the past that manual tasks would progressively be taken over by machines, but knowledge-based systems have posed more of a threat to the employment of white-collar staff engaged in rule-based paperwork. Knowledge-based systems can enable workers to manage their own productive work more effectively, for example in cell-based manufacturing. Knowledge-based systems pose a challenge to organisational cultures. There is a tendency for development and implementation to be by external consultancy, rather than through in-house expertise and broad-based participation in design. Adoption and dissemination are thus subject to the pressures of organisational politics.

BEYOND RESEARCH

It has proved difficult to sustain the momentum of research and development. Government programmes and collaborative projects have not generated the anticipated level of industrial response, and companies have been reluctant to invest heavily in a technology whose benefits take time to realise. Time has marched on, and new paradigms have captured the public imagination, including neural networks, for which grandiose claims have been made.

The world of IT has been transformed so that personal computers of considerable power have commodity status, and are sold with bundles of software packages. Users no longer expect to program as such, but to interact with a graphical user interface that allows them access to numerous applications, with intertransferability of data. Even prototype knowledge-based systems are expected to meet such standards.

Knowledge-based systems are becoming subject to the same kind of software development methods as conventional software. This can prove somewhat anomalous, as one distinguishing feature of AI programming has been its experimental and provisional nature, testing the limits rather than seeking to conform.

It has been learned that there are limits to the kinds of knowledge that can be captured in a knowledge-based system, and that the "knowledge acquisition bottleneck" is not simply something that can be cleared by a technological breakthrough. Tacit knowledge resists capture.

AN ETHICAL ENVIRONMENT

We have considered the problem of explanation once machine learning and neural networks are deployed. There are corresponding problems if organisations are left to respond to market forces without a framework of regulations, backed by enforcement measures. There needs to be an in-built system of accountability.

We arrive at the conclusion that there must be an ethical foundation for the work of organisations if disasters are to be prevented, or managed once they have occurred. Given that systems could never be complete, and individuals can never give a full account of their actions, there must be an organisational ethical environment as a matrix in which decisions can be made and acted upon. Tacit knowledge and shared beliefs are crucial if individuals are to be appropriately empowered.

How to Cause IT Disasters

In the business context, IT disasters do not simply concern technology. They derive from a basis of both business and technology, and have consequences for both. Disasters can be the means whereby dialogue begins, and phoenixes have been known to rise from ashes; however, IT disasters can be terminal for the organisation concerned.

BLAMING OTHERS

Adrian Norman [Norman 1983] has done much to demystify disasters, tracing them to human causes, including the failure to share knowledge:

"The computer professionals working on these integrity problems have generally known how to solve them in principle a generation earlier than the computer owners and users have been willing to pay for the solution." (p. ix)

Data processing is seen as an activity at a lower level than human wisdom:

"Computers process data; systems convert data into information; users of systems transform information into knowledge. But who has the wisdom to use knowledge well?" (p. x)

Despite the marketing hype, it must be accepted that computer use involves risk:

"The development and operation of computer systems is attended by risks, and these risks must either be managed or unwittingly ignored." (p. xi)

Senior managers may demand total quality and total reliability, but it is not attainable:

"Total reliability is not only impossible in theory, it would also be so expensive to pursue in practice that it could never be treated as much more than an ideal to be sought." (p. 10)

Most worrying are the limitations in the skill and training of most technical staff in the field:

"The vast majority of all data processing staff have had no professional training comparable with that required of those who practice engineering, accounting, medicine or the law." (p. 11)

Because of the novelty of information technology, we tend to suspend our critical faculties when commissioning systems:

"Corporations that would never select an architect who had never built something comparable with what they required, entrust the design of new computer systems to people whose only experience is with the systems they intend to replace. As a result computer systems that are in no way stretching the state-of-the-art exhibit the kind of failures associated with pushing at the frontiers of technology. The reluctance of corporations to make public their computer security failures reflects the fact that the great majority of such failures should have been avoided and yet were not." (p. 11)

Lessons are being learned through experience, but they are not being shared, as information is regarded as commercial in confidence. The profession is not based on a firm foundation of knowledge and experience:

"The computer profession has not yet learnt how to share its collective experience efficiently ... programmers become analysts just as they are learning to program effectively, and analysts become managers just as work was getting done by them. Meanwhile many of those who did not get promoted are still applying techniques that were being superseded two computer generations ago." (p. 22)

We should not be surprised at some of the major IT disasters that periodically generate press coverage. They must be expected in light of policy pressures:

> *"Big Systems built in a hurry are the most likely to have the biggest failures. In trying to implement their policies, governments force the administrative departments to develop systems faster than is possible without cutting some corners."* (p. 24)

Similarly, Norman is sanguine about the likely proliferation of computer abuse:

> *"A naive extrapolation of past trends suggests that as computer use penetrates ever more deeply into our lives, computer abuse will follow in line."* (p. 26)

BLAMING OURSELVES

It is not enough to criticise others for past actions that have paved the way for IT disasters. We can play our part, whether we realise it or not, by following one of a number of popular courses of action.

Business Common Sense

One of the simplest ways to cause IT disasters is to apply the conventional common-sense wisdom of modern business, taking no particular account of the nature of IT. The frequently disastrous outcome is not necessarily a consequence of technological complexity, but a reflection of management ignorance and myopia. Failure of IT projects is taken, by those who have caused the failure, as a vindication of their position, and the spiral of technological de-industrialisation continues.

Trust the Vendor

- Buy a computer system from a vendor without clearly specifying the problems that you need to solve, or the institutional context in which you are working.
- Rely on the advice of a friendly consultant or vendor without seeking a second opinion.
- Disregard talk of conformity with standards or open systems, on the grounds that the interests of your organisation must be paramount.
- If in doubt, select the cheapest option.

Delegate

- Delegate the implementation and management of the system to others who were not involved in the decision to purchase.
- Separate strategic from operational management.
- Impose quality-control standards for cosmetic purposes, ensuring a separation between operational and quality-control staff.

- Develop tightly specified job descriptions, standards and competence requirements.
- Delegate responsibility, while retaining secure financial control at the centre.
- Express information as far as possible in quantitative terms, ideally in terms of money.

Apply Financial Controls

- Apply financial controls to restrict in-house research and development in the area of information technology.
- Restrict experimental or exploratory work unless explicitly authorised and linked to achievement of goals of the core business.
- Enforce conformity with current in-house hardware and software standards.
- Ensure that accountants are in key management positions on all projects, with an eye to savings at each stage, and under instruction not to "go native". Each project or expenditure must be justified in terms of cost savings or competitive advantage for the organisation.
- There should be no attempt by operational managers to take a company-wide strategic view.

Divide and Rule

- Maintain a separation between business and information technology functions and personnel, with separate career and staff development plans.
- Enforce reporting lines through specialist functions.
- Encourage a competitive culture within the organisation, which inhibits the development of collaborative relationships.
- Reinforce this with the rigid application of performance indicators.

See Information Technology as a Tool for Finance

- Place information technology under the control of the Finance Director for reporting purposes at Board level.
- Emphasise the role of information technology in financial control, and the power available from executive information systems.
- Restrict the budget and support for executive staff development.
- Where possible remove corporate staff to a remote site.

Use Consultants

- Rely on external consultancy for specialist advice on information technology.
- Use the same consultants for management consultancy.
- Avoid the expense of appointing in-house staff to address the areas covered by the consultancy.

Set Objectives

- Set rigid financial performance objectives over the short term, such as every quarter, with a requirement for cost–benefit analysis justification of all expenditure.
- Demand that the lowest-priced bid should always be accepted in competitive tendering.
- Insist that technical supporting papers are kept commercial in confidence to prevent wider discussion.

Think Vertical

- Use information technology to support and reinforce vertical patterns of management reporting and communication.
- Maintain a strong computer centre, in charge of developing and supporting all applications.
- Enforce rigorous procedures for approval by line managers of purchases, communications and publications.
- Ensure that only standard software is used within the organisation, imposing penalties for non-compliance.

Control Information

- Restrict contacts between your staff and their opposite numbers in other departments and external organisations.
- Seek a quantifiable financial return for all information transactions.

Impose Methods

- Impose systems development methodologies, recommended by external consultants, on all departments and functions across the organisation, and oblige all to comply.
- Apply sanctions for non-compliance.

Retain Freedom to Manage

- Avoid consultation with and involvement of staff who will use or be affected by new systems.
- Ensure that management retain complete freedom to manage, dispensing with surplus staff whenever necessary.
- Inhibit communications between managers and staff, and seek to remove recognition from trade unions and professional associations.

Automate

- Automate wherever possible, replacing human employees with computer systems.
- Avoid any sentimentality in the human resource management function when shedding labour, or when considering relocating to a lower wage

environment.

- Ensure that staff, once dismissed, are removed from the organisation without delay.

Maximise Returns

- Seek to maximise shareholder returns at each stage of the process, setting a price on each information product.
- Establish clear intellectual property rights on behalf of the organisation, with signed waiver statements from all employees.

Control Communications

- Impose restrictions on the statements of employees, preventing and/or penalising criticism of company policy.
- Strengthen the public-relations and marketing functions, and prevent them from being impeded by technical staff.
- Concentrate on accentuating the positive, and avoid discussions of failures or conflicting views.

This should leave you with less of a business, and thus less exposure to IT disasters.

Technical Enthusiasm

Information technology is constantly changing and developing, and excites considerable enthusiasm. Pioneers with some technical knowledge can assemble prototype systems that promise great benefits, if only the necessary resources of time and money are made available. The resulting projects can be set unachievable objectives, which, when they are not achieved, provoke controversy, often resulting in the closure of the groups concerned. The technology advances, rather than the business.

Again a common pattern of technically led disasters can be observed.

Technical Leadership

- Find a technical enthusiast and appoint her manager in charge of the project, which may be based on her own ideas.
- Programming and software engineering skills are crucial.

Teamwork

- Give the enthusiastic manager the budget she asks for, and the team members she has chosen.
- Ensure that the team is technically autonomous and self-sufficient.

Plan

- Ask the manager to define her objectives, and to identify the milestone stages that she will achieve *en route* to her goal.
- Demand a full specification from the outset, in terms of deliverables, tasks and sub-tasks to which strict adherence will be required.

Autonomy

- Insulate the project group from the rest of the organisation and give it financial autonomy.

Resources

- Provide further resources on request by the project manager, without involving other managers in the organisation.

Modifications

- Extend deadlines and modify milestones on request by the project manager, in response to technical arguments.

Equipment

- Provide new-generation, non-standard, equipment for the project team on request, ensuring that the team maintains a position abreast of the state of the art.

Not Invented Here

- Encourage the project team to develop their own software tools and environment, rather than using proprietary packages.

Prototype

- Develop working systems before consulting potential users.

Outsource

- Buy an externally produced product, if it is cheaper, and close down the in-house technical function.
- Take advice from a systems integrator who can sell you proprietary systems, re-engineer your business and take on the outsourcing of your IT needs.

Mission Orientation

Major technology projects require major management frameworks, with implications for finance and decision-making. Such programmes frequently straddle the public and private sectors, bringing together different management cultures and technical perspectives. The objectives are often couched in general, apparently socially comprehensible, terms, but may not include consideration of market demands. "Technology push" prevails over "applications pull", except in key focus areas intended to "pull through" the technology for wider applications use. Projects often involve a number of organisations on different sites. The collaboration may be successful at the human and technical level, but without clear short- or medium-term commercial benefits.

There is now sufficient experience of managed mission-based projects to discern common approaches.

Man on the Moon

- Define a target objective, such as a speech-driven workstation, and design a project structure to deliver the product over an extended specified period of time.

Men Across Sites

- Sub-projects should be established to deal with separate technical areas, each involving technical experts, probably from different organisations, working on different sites.

Desk Research

- Conduct a literature and technology search in terms of the goals of the project, using specialist monitoring teams.

Mock-Ups

- Build simulation systems that model the target states of key technologies, as environments in which particular problems can be addressed.

Bureaucracy

- Establish a long-term financial programme and management structure, empowered to sustain the project through the initial years of inevitable expenditure rather than financial return.

Uncles

- Encourage academic research that contributes to the defined objectives of the programme; by implication, discourage academic research with less apparent applicability.

Spin-Off

- Look for commercially exploitable by-products of the programme in the early years, with a view to attracting revenue and raising awareness of the technical direction of the longer-term project.

Demonstration

- Commission a succession of demonstrator projects to test the emerging technology.

Champions

- Identify product champions to spearhead development and dissemination of the new technology.

Awareness

- Convene regular workshops and conferences to share knowledge derived from the programme.

Termination

- Terminate the programme when funds are exhausted, and move on to a new technology and new set of initiatives.

A Proliferation of Paradigms

The three models outlined above are not mutually exclusive, and individual participants or groups may see their involvement in different terms. It is understandable if different people in an organisation concerned with solving problems in common start with different perceptions, and feel they work within different paradigms. It is unreasonable to expect these differences to disappear when use is made of computer systems: it is more likely that technical complexity will make most participants lose touch with their particular standpoint and feel under pressure to accept the overall outcome. The solution may unravel if the outcome is deemed to be unacceptable and explanations are required, with each person needing an explanation in their own terms, couched in the language of their initial paradigm.

Individual and Collective Views

To some extent, participation in an organisation entails the submergence of individual positions in favour of adherence to the collective whole, but there is normally some assumption of transparency in the means by which this is accomplished, some auditable trail of accountability. As with democratic decision-making, this can work well on the small scale; but, with increased size and complexity, full explanation of decisions, except in terms of the institution or organisation itself, becomes impossible.

Complexity and Ignorance

On this argument, IT disasters can be special cases of organisational disasters brought about by complexity. Naive faith in, or cynical adherence to, bureaucratic procedures can be reinforced by the introduction of IT, which offers a reinforcing layer of obfuscation to baffle all but the most discerning.

In the case of IT, the problem goes further. People can use IT systems based on particular paradigms without, in the technical sense, knowing what they are doing. For most users of advanced windowing systems this will be the case, where users can manipulate spreadsheets or other formalisms in ignorance of underlying models. Graphics workstations supporting knowledge engineering environments may offer an integration of logic programming, frame-based reasoning and object orientation, with a sophistication of user interface that protects the user from consideration of the code used in computation. Amid such complexity, the user loses control; once lost, it cannot be regained.

Historical and Technical Perspectives

2

Editorials bemoan the failure of business software, and often conclude that the answer is simply to complain. There is evidence of Boardroom frustration, complicated by ignorance. The following editorial appeared in *Business and Technology Magazine*, September 1994:

"If the Severn Bridge collapsed, there would be a major public outcry. The structural engineer responsible would be hung, drawn and quartered and then thrown into the Avon. Fortunately such disasters very rarely happen. There is a reason, and it is a simple one. The companies concerned know that it is not acceptable for them to make mistakes.

Why then can software companies get away with producing so much substandard software? There is no reason why software bugs should exist. Programming is as precise a science as engineering, and just as bridges can be tested for stresses and strains, sophisticated software testing programs are available to ensure that a manufacturer does not let any bugs creep into the final code before the product is released. After all, if you buy a Golf GTi you do not expect the steering wheel to come off in your hands when you are doing 70 mph down the M4. So why should we accept shoddy databases that crash without warning or reason?

Unfortunately, the business community has come to accept software defects as a way of life. We re-start our PCs without a moment's hesitation. How many times have you pulled the plug knowing that three hours' work is down the plug-hole? Far too often, it is time for major corporate users to stand up and be counted. Only when the industry realises that users will not accept defective products will they take the time to iron out bugs before flogging their products to the punters.

> *To add insult to injury, many of these software companies now expect us to pay increasing amounts of cash for customer support. Very often this 'support' is only required because the software doesn't work in the first place, or because a feature is underdocumented.*
>
> *How do we get these software giants to take notice? Irate telephone calls are all very well, but shouting at some Customer Support Executive is about as effective as complaining about price increases to the check-out girl at Sainsbury's. So the next time your accounts department tell you that there's a hundred records missing from the sales database because of a software problem, tell them to contact the legal department.*
>
> *It's time for change. It's time to sue."*

Before suing, it may be worth understanding the nature of the problem.

Single Technology Solutions

There has been a tendency to seek to apply a single technology solution to a wide range of problems. Enthusiastic business users of information technology have concluded that it offers the solution to all their problems, even though their understanding of both the problems and the technology is limited.

The consultants Ingersoll Engineers reported on flexible manufacturing systems [Ingersoll 1982]:

> *"The main surprise was that so many problems were born of a naivety among managers and engineers alike in their apparent belief that the task is relatively simple and all that is needed is money, a hardware vendor and a group of parts to be made."*

This has not been the approach of the leading figures in the development of computer science, who have retained a healthy and informed scepticism. Edsger Dijkstra has been a constant critic of conventional approaches, and has highlighted the difference between what is understood and what is attempted. As he wrote in his "Notes on structured programming" [Dijkstra 1972]:

> *"Widespread underestimation of the specific difficulties of size seems one of the major underlying causes of the current software failure."* (p. 2)

True computer professionals will, Dijkstra argues, remain conscious of their deficiencies:

> *"As a slow-witted human being I have a very small head and I had better learn to live with it and to respect my limitations and give them full credit, rather than to try to ignore them, for the latter vain effort will be punished by failure."*

The problem is that key decisions are made by those with less understanding of technology. Dijkstra was concerned about the degree of confidence of users:

"Present day computers are amazing pieces of equipment, but most amazing of all are the uncertain grounds on account of which we attach any validity to their output. It starts already with our belief that the hardware functions properly."
(p. 3)

This problem is not a new one. Charles Babbage found the atmosphere in the 1830s extremely frustrating when he was seeking to develop the first computers. He complained of a lack of general understanding of technical complexity, in a letter to Edward, Duke of Somerset [Babbage 1833]. He singled out Government for particular criticism:

"I have ... been compelled to perceive that of all countries England is that in which there exists the greatest number of practical engineers who can appreciate the mechanical part whilst at the same time it is of all others that country in which the governing powers are most incompetent to understand the merit either of the mechanical or mathematical."

Babbage noted that complex processes would require a longer period of learning. He wrote, in his *On the Economy of Machinery and Manufactures* [Babbage 1835]:

"Of the time required for learning. It will readily be admitted, that the portion of time occupied in the acquisition of any art will depend on the difficulty of its execution; and that the greater the number of distinct processes, the longer will be the time which the apprentice must employ in acquiring it."

Dijkstra [1972] confirms that programming meets harsh business reality when it comes to dealing with complexity:

"The art of programming is the art of organising complexity." *(p. 6)*

Computers are not just administrative tools, but pose serious challenges to all thinking managers, transforming their whole working environment.

"The influence of computers as tools might turn out to be but a ripple on the surface of our culture, whereas I expect them to have a much more profound influence in their capacity of intellectual challenge." *(p. 10)*

When difficulties arise, those with specialist knowledge are faced with awkward decisions. When the Emperor has no clothes, this must be pointed out:

"Sometimes we discover unpleasant truths. Whenever we do so, we are in difficulties. Suppressing them is scientifically dishonest, so we must tell them, but telling them, however, will fire back on us. If the truths are sufficiently unpalatable, our audience is psychically incapable of accepting them, and we will be written off as totally unrealistic, hopelessly idealistic, dangerously revolutionary, foolishly gullible, or what have you."

It is becoming apparent that programming requires mathematical skills of the highest order, despite the popular perception that new technology has made programming accessible to all. Increasingly it is assumed that such skills are no longer needed, but the fundamental issues remain unchanged:

"Programming is one of the most difficult branches of applied mathematics; the poorer mathematicians had better remain pure mathematicians."

The users of powerful computing tools are not unchanged by the experience, and may come to deal with new levels of problem:

"The tools we use have a profound (and devious!) influence on our thinking habits, and ... on our thinking abilities."

On the other hand, the mass use of computers means that the typical user, characterised by shallow and short-term thinking, is not capable of making best use of the technology. Such a user cannot meet the challenges of business IT without a sound educational background:

"The problems of business administration in general and data base management in particular are much too difficult for people that think in computerese, compounded with sloppy English."

Technology cannot necessarily be enlisted in support of simplistic management approaches. No matter what resources are thrown at a problem, it may resist solution:

"About the use of language: it is impossible to sharpen a pencil with a blunt axe. It is equally vain to try to do it with ten blunt axes instead."

It was a false move to rely on the strength of major vendors, though it seemed uncontroversial in business terms:

"Many companies that have made themselves dependent on the equipment of a certain major manufacturer (and in so doing have sold their soul to the devil) will collapse under the sheer weight of the unmastered complexity of their data processing systems."

Describing the working of computer systems in "user-friendly" terms, as is now happening with personal-computer operating systems, can itself be dangerous [Dijkstra 1982]:

"The use of anthropomorphic terminology when dealing with computing systems is a symptom of professional immaturity."

There are serious implications for the education and development of future professionals, who will work in a very demanding commercial environment:

"Even if we know how to educate tomorrow's professional programmer, it is not certain that the society we are living in will allow us to do so." (p. 30)

This is no longer a problem restricted to professionals, for the technology has proliferated and become omnipresent [Dijkstra 1972]:

"As long as there were no machines, programming was no problem at all; when we had a few weak computers, programming became a mild problem, and now that we

have gigantic computers, programming has become an equally gigantic problem. In this sense the electronics industry has solved not a single problem, it has only created them – it has created the problem of using its products."

In short, the founding fathers of computing are profoundly concerned about the naive faith placed in their fallible technology by a new short-termist and uneducated generation of users.

Tools

A child learns the use of language and toys in an experimental manner; for many senior executives the arrival of IT in the office and on the desktop offers a second childhood, but without the protective presence of Mummy or Nanny. Today's senior Board members may have been sent away to boarding school in their youth, learning basic social skills at minimum risk to the family home and reputation.

Computer vendors have recognised the appeal of second childhood in the way they have packaged computer games with standard hardware: many managers spend Christmas near the computer ostensibly helping their children. The intelligent ones among them will have been learning from their children.

Managers must learn from their children, and senior managers from their grandchildren. Just as children are more adept at programming video recorders, children who have grown up in the world of computers find the technology holds few terrors for them, though they know little of the world. Harold Thimbleby, Professor of Information Technology at Stirling University, explored this phenomenon for *New Scientist* on 23rd February 1991 [Thimbleby 1991], freely confessing that he was baffled by such consumer electronic technology.

Thimbleby concluded that video-cassette recorders are hard to use because:

- The problems are not obvious to technically minded designers.
- Designers tend to add one or two new features per model.
- Finding problems is easy, but fixing them is hard.
- Manufacturers continue to be allowed to get away with it.

He argued that, instead, certain simple principles of good design practice should be observed:

- Make frequent tasks easy, and less frequent ones harder.
- Make the mode of use consistent.
- Every action should have a reaction.
- Designers should free themselves from history.

Such principles have rarely been followed by designers, who have seen their technology as fundamentally new.

The distinguished artificial intelligence researchers Minsky and Papert at MIT concentrated on educational lessons from programming, including the value of debugging as a means of learning from one's own mistakes. Minsky wrote, in his Turing Award Lecture [Minsky 1969; in ACM 1987]:

"To help people learn is to help them build, in their heads, various kinds of computational models. This can be done by a teacher who has, in his own head, a reasonable model of what is in the pupil's head.

For the same reason, the student, when debugging his own model and procedures, should have a model of what he is doing, and must know good debugging techniques, such as how to formulate simple but critical test cases.

It will help the student to know something about computational models and programming."

Artificial intelligence was concerned with this critical area, clarifying ideas through the experimental development of programs.

Papert wrote, in his *Mindstorms* [Papert 1980], of his excitement at the discovery of systems, and of how:

"Gears, serving as models, carried many otherwise abstract ideas into my head."

He argued that:

"You can be the gear, you can understand how it turns by projecting yourself into its place and turning with it."

"In my vision, the child programs the computer and, in doing so, both acquires a sense of mastery over a piece of the most modern and powerful technology and establishes an intimate contact with some of the deepest ideas from science, from mathematics, and from the art of intellectual model building."

Innovative business cultures require a toleration of failure, provided that lessons can be learned. The objective of "getting it right first time, every time", except when the process concerned is itself simply repetition rather than innovation, can be destructive of progress and business success.

Keeping IT Simple

Simplicity is a commendable principle, but it can be dangerously illusory. Pandering to current prejudices by allowing an extension to current practices may be at the expense of longer-term objectives and developments that require a change of direction. Abelson [1973] offered an observation from his experience of social psychology:

"Most of the worst inter- and intra-national conflicts of the world are greatly exacerbated by the human penchant for interposing oversimplified symbol systems between themselves and the external world."

Working with Colby [Colby and Abelson 1973] he demonstrated the potential for disaster in a memorable account of the working of the "Ideology Machine", which could automatically respond to questions in the manner of an American Cold War Warrior. Written at the time of the Goldwater Presidential Campaign, it gives an uncannily accurate summary of the White House style of the Reagan Presidency.

Colby and Abelson demystify politics by such example systems. There is a need to similarly demystify computing and computer science, so that managers and decision-makers have some understanding of what computers are doing on their behalf. It is all too easy to be beguiled by the commercial package, not asking what is going on behind the scenes. Having used a computer in a particular way, the easiest choice is to continue, adding an additional feature or function to what is already known.

Simplicity at the interface for the user may involve intricacy and ingenuity behind the scenes for the system developer and support team. It may also encourage the user to believe that the technology is, and will continue to be, simple. At some stage there is likely to be discontinuity, and this requires management and preparation.

Bench-Capon and McEnery [1989] argue that we should see computers as communication systems, facilitating human interaction, in particular between programmers and users. Too much attention is given to computer systems in themselves, they argue, when the issue should be the communication between the people concerned:

"It is the programmer who should be modelling potential users, and the programmer that the users should be modelling; the computer system is properly viewed only as the passive medium of communication, like the board on which a notice is printed."

When things go wrong, the tendency is to blame the computer system. Philosophically, this is incoherent, for, as they point out:

"The system does not have any intentions, and if the user attempts to define them the user is committing the pathetic fallacy of anthropomorphising the system, and such a mistake can only produce error rather than insight."

The more the computer system appears tailored for the particular circumstances, or even endowed with intelligence, the more dangerous the situation may be:

"The more the phrases presented by the computer are adapted to the specific situation, the more the user may be tempted to think them adapted to each user, and so read into them meanings that would have been recognised as inappropriate in a book or conventional system."

Hopson [1993] has described the role of the power user, providing the facilities for what he calls the human user interface:

"What the voluntary sector hacker does is to customise and tailor systems so that 'real' users, ordinary computer-disinterested people, can get from the machine what they or their organisation require. The need for this role arises because all off-the-peg software applications are generic in nature. None are designed for or dedicated to a single task, so they do nothing very well. Even to write something as simple as a letter using a word-processing package will require a fair amount of software setting up before it can be done well, and time after time in a consistent house style.

It is the power user, or hacker, who builds document templates, writes macros, designs menus, creates batch routines etc. These things then sit as the real 'front-end' between the everyday user of the system and the technology of hardware, operating system and software.

The front-end is a distillation of a power user's skill and knowledge batched up as meta-functions of the environment that is being used. Front-ends are designed to do what your hacker would do if he or she were constantly available at the beck and call of anyone who sat down at a keyboard, or picked up a mouse. In brief, what can often be found in voluntary organisations are prototypical expert systems – where the domain specialism is that of knowing how to use a computer 'properly' and achieve desired results."

This is a much more complex picture than that suggested by commercial software vendors. It suggests that, despite advances in technology, human expertise remains critical for successful use of computer applications by non-specialist users.

The Emperor's Old Clothes

In Tony Hoare's version of the Hans Christian Andersen fairy story, told in his Turing Award Lecture [Hoare 1980; in ACM 1987], the tailor's new clothes are put on top of the previous layers of clothing already worn by the Emperor. The choice of clothes was made on the basis of the promised features and extensions. Beneath all the layers of clothes the Emperor had slipped away to a more congenial life elsewhere, leaving the clothes free-standing and empty.

Hoare's targets in the world of computing included the American programming language ADA, imposed as a standard by the US Department of Defense, and enormously complicated, full of additional features. His criticisms are aimed at managers, and have profound implications:

"You know what went wrong? ... You let your programmers do things which you yourself do not understand."

Managers need to be able to provide clear specifications if they are to achieve successful working systems:

"A lack of clarity in specification is one of the surest signs of a deficiency in the program it describes, and the two faults must be removed simultaneously before the project is embarked upon."

Hoare has issued clear warnings, on the dangers of software pollution, the spread of unreliable software employed on ever more critical functions, which are echoed by Manny Lehman [1985]:

"An unreliable programming language generating unreliable programs constitutes a far greater risk to our environment and to our society than unsafe cars, toxic pesticides or accidents at nuclear power stations."

He is sceptical of the claims of software engineers, seeing emptiness at the heart of many of their projects [Hoare 1980]:

"The tailor is canonised as the patron saint of all consultants, because in spite of the enormous fees that he extracted, he was never able to convince his clients of his dawning realisation that their clothes have no emperor."

He was similarly sceptical of the claims of logic programming at the time of enthusiasm for fifth-generation computers, and developed the new language OCCAM as a means of highlighting the basic concepts behind computation, as distinct from traditional sequential computation on von Neumann machines.

Gries [1991] expressed similar views, pointing to the deficiencies of specifications and software engineering professional practice:

"In large corporations, one can find many instances of software written from poorly prepared requirements and specifications, where a more professional engineering practice would have been to rewrite the specification completely before beginning design and development." (p. 46)

He sees software engineers as lacking in both judgement and responsibility:

"Many software engineers lack the judgement to determine whether their task is well defined, or at least the sense of responsibility and confidence to complain when it is not well defined." (p. 46)

Such a view does not inspire one to confidence in software engineers, whose systems have become fundamental to the success and survival of an increasing proportion of organisations.

Human-Centred Systems

Human-centred systems provide an alternative paradigm for systems development, and derive from a critique of conventional systems. Mike Cooley has argued [Cooley 1990]:

"We are now at an historical turning point, when decisions we make in respect of the new technologies will have a profound effect upon the way we relate to each other, to our work, and even to nature itself. By failing to criticise and analyse the systems now being introduced, we may fail to perceive the opportunities for alternative systems that are of a more human-centred variety."

Cooley echoes Karl Marx's concern with the division of labour and the alienation of the worker from the production process, what Marx described in *Das Kapital* as:

"… the separation of the intellectual powers of production from manual labour, and the conversion of those powers into the might of capital over labour."

Cooley has identified the European cultural tradition from which human-centred systems have emerged:

"In recent years there has been a growing tendency to assume that there is only one form of technology: that which we may now think of as 'American technology'. A richer and more sensitive way to view new technology would be to perceive it as a cultural product, and since culture has produced different languages, different music and different literature, why should it not produce different forms of technology, forms which reflect the cultural, historical, economic and ideological aspirations of the society which will use them? Should there not be a form of European technology reflecting European aspirations (if more in the rhetoric than in the reality) of motivation, self-activism, dignity of the individual, concern for quality etc., and reflecting also the reality of the European manufacturing base which is composed predominantly of medium-sized and small-scale units?"

Cooley identifies problems with the current direction of computer technology, as the involvement of people is reduced while systems gain in sophistication:

"We may be about to repeat, in the field of intellectual work, many of the mistakes we made at such enormous cost at earlier historical stages when skilled manual work was subjected to the introduction of high-capital equipment. Seventy years of scientific management have seen the fragmentation of skills grind through the spectrum of workshop activity, engulfing even the most creative and satisfying manual tasks such as that of tool-making. Throughout that period, most industrial laboratories, design offices and administrative centres were the sanctuary of the conceptual, planning and administrative aspects of work. In those areas, one spur to output was a dedication to the task in hand, an interest in it and the satisfaction of dealing with a job from start to finish."

To lose the involvement and commitment of the human worker is to court disaster. This argument has been developed by those applying human-centred approaches to business [Corbett *et al.* 1991; Kaura and Ennals 1993; Ainger *et al.* 1995].

THE NEED FOR HUMAN-CENTRED SYSTEMS

Weizenbaum, in his book *Computer Power and Human Reason* [Weizenbaum 1972], highlighted the dangers that will surround an uncritical acceptance of computerised techniques. Weizenbaum had previously caught the imagination of the public with his ELIZA [Weizenbaum 1966], an interactive dialogue program that simulated the responses of a Rogerian psychoanalyst. The interest was, however, short-lived, once the program was explained. He was concerned to demystify computers, and argued that:

> "To explain is to explain away ... once a particular program is unmasked, once its inner workings are explained in language sufficiently plain to induce understanding, its magic crumbles away; it stands revealed as a mere collection of procedures, each quite comprehensible."

Weizenbaum's critique turned the attention away from the computer to the user and the organisation:

> "The computer has long been a solution looking for problems – the ultimate technological fix which insulates us from having to look at problems ... Devices that shield us from having to come into contact with fellow human beings are rapidly taking over much of our daily lives."

He argued that the spread of IT could in itself turn into a disaster:

> "Increasing computerisation may well allow us to increase the productivity of labour indefinitely, but to produce what? More video games and fancier television sets along with 'smarter' weapons? And with people's right to feed their families and themselves largely conditional on them 'working', how do we provide for those whose work has been taken away from them by machines? The vision of production with hardly any human effort, of the consumption of every product imaginable, may excite the greed of a society whose appetites are fixed on things."

Cooley [1990] argued that it was time to consider alternative ways of using the technology:

> "Given the scale and nature of these problems, and the exponential rate of technological change within which they are located, it behoves all of us to seek to demonstrate that alternatives exist which reject neither human judgement, tacit knowledge, intuition and imagination nor the scientific or rule-based method. We should rather unite them in a symbiotic totality."

Human-centred systems can be presented as being more efficient than conventional fully automated systems because the operators can use their skills and experience, with the aid of powerful software tools. Such systems are more economical because they are designed to be more efficient, more flexible, have a higher take-up time, lower running cost, cost less to buy and take less time to commission. We could ask why this approach is not already dominant: the answer has much to do with human relationships and management methods.

Executive Information Systems

There is an illuminating contrast with executive information systems, which bring information technology to a new group of users who are both ill-informed and highly placed. EIS technology promises to place financial information at the fingertips of those with a control and monitoring function, safely insulated from the working environment from which the information has been derived.

Matthews [in Holtham 1992] introduces executive information systems in the context of corporate policy, and considers insights from EIS into the way the organisation adds value. He suggests that the question to ask in designing an EIS is: "What information would potential predators most like to have about your organisation?"

EIS have been used in the introduction of "Total Quality" in London Underground, adding power to customer–supplier chains in order to effect organisational change. British Airways introduced the Airline Information Management System (AIMS), with support from the highest corporate level. The HOLOS system in British Telecom emphasises the needs of top managers.

More case studies are provided in Rolph and Bartram [1992]. Companies such as Sun, Boots and British Airways justify their investments in EIS in terms of improved understanding of the business, and offer practical approaches to implementation, as well as examples of Chief Executives who are regular users of EIS.

The spread of EIS systems highlights what was seen as the need for hybrid managers, competent in both business and information technology; the normal British Computer Society definition of a hybrid amounts to a job description for an executive information system project leader.

Culture, Competence and Complexity

3

The Demands of the Modern Economy

The future of a modern industrial economy depends to a significant extent on the strength of its manufacturing industry, and the skills of the workforce. There is a temptation, particularly on the part of politicians and senior managers, to demand clear and rapid change, and an increase in the number of qualifications awarded.

If we take account of the changing nature of work and of technology, and the increased dependence on knowledge, we may arrive at a somewhat different conclusion. We argue for a broader approach, which gives due attention to the tacit knowledge of the worker and the culture of working life [Göranzon and Josefson 1988; Göranzon and Florin 1990, 1991, 1992]. This argument applies for unskilled, semi-skilled, skilled and professional workers, including managers. There are many lessons to be learned from international experience, as each company and national economy has to compete at an international level.

RESPONSES TO BRITISH ECONOMIC DECLINE

The last century has seen a decline in the relative economic position of the United Kingdom, from a position of technical and commercial leadership to one of reduced ambitions, where it has become clear that a small island cannot hope to dominate in each field. Limited natural resources, as is the case with Japan, mean that knowledge-based industries have critical importance. Even in areas where leadership is not maintained, it is vital to retain core competences and understanding, in order to make intelligent use of technologies derived from others. At the company level, it cannot be acceptable to be dependent on imported technology that remains mysterious to managers and workforce.

In the United Kingdom, widespread dissatisfaction with industrial performance, especially in manufacturing industry, and disillusion with standards in
education and training, has led Government to develop a new competence-based
approach, which in turn has stimulated the publication of controversial reports
[Moser 1993; Smithers 1993]. There is general agreement that competitive
advantage depends on strengthening the knowledge and skills of the workforce
at all levels; true flexibility in the workforce requires a stronger set of transferable skills, including mastery of new technologies. A major obstacle is finance,
at a time of cost reduction and restraints in public spending. Improvements in
training and education involve major investment expenditure, with a long pay-
back period. Companies have yet to accept the concept of support and
maintenance for their workforce as a priority investment.

IN SEARCH OF COMPETENCE

British Government policy has been to increase the emphasis on competence-
based qualifications as opposed to traditional academic modes of study and
assessment. Inappropriate academic courses, detached from the practical needs
of industry, were blamed for deficiencies in training at all levels. The National
Council for Vocational Qualifications was established by Government [Judd
1993] to construct a national system of qualifications covering the full breadth of
industry and employment areas, and all levels up to and including postgraduate
professional qualifications. The new system was designed to replace the previous
mass of diverse qualifications derived from inconsistent standards, and was also
intended to place training under the direction of senior private-sector industry
managers.

Working with a set of Industry Lead Bodies comprising representatives of
employers in different employment sectors, a process of Taylorist decomposition
has been carried out on complex tasks, breaking them down into manageable
sub-tasks, in order to identify the key competences that are necessary for
efficient performance of standard tasks, to be assessed against agreed criteria.
The criteria themselves derive from the study of the performance of current
workers. Occupations have been classified in a manner corresponding to the
Registrar-General's long-established Classification of Social Class, and Vocational Qualifications are currently being developed and standardised for a growing proportion of lower-level occupations, covering craft and technician-level
work.

Frequently the qualifications are to be awarded on the basis of a portfolio of
Prior Experiential Learning, giving long-overdue credit for learning acquired by
experience. This, together with the widespread use of open and distance learning, removes the need for costly absence from work in order to study, but
necessitates new and complex processes of verification. Government and
management are attracted by the prospect of a relatively painless transition to a
highly skilled workforce.

STANDARDS AND CONTROL

Industry and professional bodies have responded with some confusion. The Government claims that standards for vocational qualifications are being set by industrial employers via Industry Lead Bodies, but employers remain distant and bemused, denying "ownership" and responsibility. Professional bodies (including lawyers, personnel managers and engineers) fear an assault on their status and power if their own qualifications are required to be accredited against externally imposed standards. Engineering Examination Boards remain attached to traditional qualifications, and seek to withhold recognition from University engineering courses that deviate from traditional entry requirements. Professional expertise and status is in question, with the autonomy and very survival of the traditional professional bodies in question.

There is an issue of control. Governments can determine the form and function of bodies and agencies over which it has financial control. This means in Britain that Universities, Colleges of Further Education, Training and Enterprise Councils, and awarding bodies such as the Business and Technician Education Council, together with the National Council for Vocational Qualifications, have little choice but to conform if they are to stay in existence. The overall system, established in the name of free-market capitalism, boasts a degree of central control and State planning of which Stalin and his GOSPLAN agency would have been jealous.

A CULTURAL DIVIDE

In Britain few politicians, or their Senior Civil Servants, have a background in engineering, science or technology. An arts background has traditionally been the route to success in the professions of accountancy and law, and in business and management. Even in manufacturing industry, it has not been assumed that managers will have experience, or understanding, of the processes they are managing. This is replicated across the Civil Service, including Civil Servants responsible for vocational education and training. Training has been considered something for lower-level staff, planned by their superiors. The class system is very much alive.

SKILL WITHOUT PRICE

To the extent that traditional industrial skills are still required, it has been assumed that they can be expressed in terms of specific competences, for which employees can receive specific on-the-job training, without requiring lengthy and expensive apprenticeship or formal education. Such skilled employees would increasingly be contracted on a casual (or flexible) basis, rather than developing long-term expertise. Thus we have seen the growth of self-employment, and the reduction of trade union involvement in working life. Where public-sector work is subjected to compulsory competitive tendering, there is pressure to accept the lowest bid, which involves the greatest degradation of wages and conditions, and reductions in standards of health and safety. Costs are reduced: that is enough for the accountants. Skill and culture do not carry price labels. Their value is highlighted by their absence: a frequent conclusion of reports following disasters.

Challenging Professionals

Just as trade unions were considered to pose a challenge to Government power in the 1970s and 1980s, justifying legislative reforms, professionals are now under pressure to conform. In a free-market economy, where cutting costs is a primary objective, why should wasteful expenditure be devoted to education and training beyond the minimum required to secure competent performance of standard tasks? Why should the economy, and employers, be held hostage to the excessive and exorbitant demands of professionals and their professional bodies for protracted periods of study, and obliged to tolerate the arcane rituals of professional education and institutional practice? In the United Kingdom this question has been asked of teachers, doctors, nurses, firemen, police officers, ambulance men and women, and prison officers: it is hardly surprising that the same challenges are being posed to engineers and managers. Professional bodies are considering their response: will they comply or resist? Resistance may mean the loss of public funding and the removal of official recognition, including places at the table of national discussions.

Engineering as a Form of Life

Engineering, including software engineering, is a complex form of life, in which experienced practitioners have accumulated a mass of knowledge of different kinds [Cooley 1989; Rosenbrock 1989], including the modes of interaction with other professionals. Each artefact or tool embodies the skills of the maker: indeed, the traditional craftsman would as a matter of course make his own tools. In so doing, over the period of apprenticeship and employment as a journeyman, he would develop an awareness of strengths, tolerances, and variations from standard designs and constructions.

Formation as an engineer would involve the development and exercise of a range of skills, applied and refined under supervision over time. Understanding and experience of physical objects was critical, going beyond the realms of "book learning".

WHAT IS AN ENGINEER?

As John Monk of the Open University has pointed out [Monk 1993], the typical graduate engineer is not directly engaged in the manufacturing process: his products tend to be designs and reports rather than physical objects. However, the designs and reports only derive their meaning from their relationship with the world of physical objects, and their formulations in language and symbols that are comprehended and used by the managers who constitute their audience. This suggests that the engineer must develop expertise in a complex process of knowledge representation and mediation, maintaining dialogue with the client or commissioning manager regarding the transformation of physical objects within the terms of an agreed specification, and recording objectives and progress in a variety of media. This requires practice, rather than just theory.

In modern economic and industrial conditions, it makes little sense to adhere to a traditional technocentric approach to engineering systems, where systems are regarded as complete and humans play a relatively subordinate role. Engineering efficiency and effectiveness will be enhanced if managers and workers can address technology in their own terms, recognising their role as active agents in systems that operate in a world of uncertainty and incomplete information. This was the fundamental motivation behind the work of Deming [1982] on quality.

As Brodner [1990, 1995] has demonstrated in his work on anthropocentric systems in production engineering, the adoption of a new engineering culture has had a transforming effect on quality, the time taken to develop and bring to market new models, and levels of work satisfaction. Empowering workers at cell level on the factory floor, as Kaura and Ennals [1993] have shown, enhances manufacturing efficiency and effectiveness while changing working relationships and management structures across the company.

In a context where human interaction and the shared interpretation of reports and designs are critical, it is somewhat anomalous if the emphasis of engineering education is overwhelmingly scientific, to the exclusion of insights from the humanities and philosophy. Engineers are actors in the world of business, organisations and politics [Corbett *et al.* 1991], and need access to insights from both acting and the social sciences, much of which is best achieved through practice and reflection.

Competence and Professional Education

WORKERS BY HAND AND BRAIN

The traditional distinction between work by hand and by brain has been falsely drawn, as Cooley has argued [Cooley 1989]. Cooley points to the division between architects and builders in the construction of late Renaissance cathe-drals, and has highlighted the dangers of designers working on components without proper understanding of their use. The present generation of com-puter technology permits us to end such arbitrary divisions of labour. The same engineer can both think and produce products. The manager can take an active part in production. Their roles and status, however, may be radically changed.

In a society that makes no verbal distinction between the shop-floor mechanic and the graduate professional, calling both "engineers", the subtleties and rituals of the engineering culture have not been recognised. The status of the British graduate engineer has suffered, by comparison with Japanese, German or French counterparts.

Instead, a Taylorist taxonomy of competences and standards has been offered, allowing the individual to claim competence in sub-tasks at any level on demand, and factoring out consideration of underlying knowledge and understanding, including craft and tacit knowledge. The competence approach offers cost savings, by declaring attendance at expensive courses superfluous as long as competence can be demonstrated in the performance of specified tasks.

THE IMPACT OF COMPUTERS

The development of high-power, but low-cost, computing systems has further blurred understanding of skills. Increasingly, manufacturing employees are required to mind machines, enabling unskilled staff to produce high-technology products, but leaving them impotent if the machines malfunction. Production continuity is greatly aided if workers understand the reasons for system break-downs, and are empowered to take action to resolve problems. This implies a breadth and depth of technical knowledge that has become rarer, as skilled workers have been replaced by machines.

Monk [1993] is right to note that, although computers have changed the work of the engineer, they do not make the engineer redundant:

"People are still needed to think about questions of reliability, safety and acceptability; people bring to bear experience, tradition, experiment and theory in answering these questions and making judgements about the contradictory evidence. How things are weighed up is affected by the culture in which the activity is taking place. This is not a task for computers."

Unfortunately, executive decisions are often made at Board level by managers who lack the necessary knowledge and understanding. Their use of the computer flows from their perception of the management task: the computer is merely the tool, a flawed management system is to blame. As Corbett [1989] has pointed out, managers need to ensure that the systems they manage are providing learning experience for those on whose judgement the organisation will depend:

"A system which does not provide the experience out of which craft skill can develop will be vulnerable in those circumstances when human intervention becomes necessary."

This whole argument applies to the problem of IT management, which has been seen as an assemblage of detailed skills, acquired piecemeal, rather than a complex environment requiring the development of knowledge and understanding over time.

PROFESSIONAL EDUCATION

In what some have called the "third culture" [Ennals and Gardin 1990; Göranzon 1995], we reject the over-rigid demarcation between arts and social sciences on the one hand, and natural sciences and technology on the other. We see science and technology as being conducted in a cultural context, and applied with the priority given to human need. While rejecting a narrow anthropocentric view of the world, which can have damaging implications for the environment and other species, we see humans at the centre of systems, rather than technology. We regard technological systems as implementations of ideologies, and to be treated with similar caution: systems are based on models of reality, often with arbitrary approaches to quantification, and they can never be relied on as substitutes for human judgement.

Engineers, including knowledge engineers, will need to play a central role in this "third culture", but this will require reforms in engineering education. In turn, this requires changes in the broader educational and political system.

Narrow vocationalism is destructive of a common culture, and serves only the interests of a ruling elite, typically drawn from a background in the arts. Once professional skills have been destroyed, whether through automation or narrow vocationalism, it is not clear that they can be rebuilt: whole professions can vanish, never to return.

We may identify common classes of concern across the professions, and see the case for new cross-disciplinary and international courses, which may serve to enhance solidarity and mutual understanding.

CRITICS AS ENGINEERS

Engineers are frequently called upon to write consultancy reports on the working of particular systems, or to compare and contrast alternative solutions to specified problems. A professional vocabulary of critical language has developed, together with a reference set of cases that can be used as benchmarks of quality. We can identify styles and traditions, techniques and devices, which may be more or less integrated, well conceived and appropriate to the needs of the user.

We can thus see engineers as critics for part of their work, but we may encounter more apparently principled resistance when we talk of critics as engineers. Many critics like to stand back from the phenomena they describe, reluctant to acknowledge their presence in the systems or cultural products under study. They point to their experience and technical expertise, but fail to notice the corresponding characteristics of engineers, with whom they may have little social discourse. Even in literary circles, it is relatively rare for the same writer to be respected as critic and creative writer, such as Malcolm Bradbury, novelist [Bradbury 1992] and critic of the novel [Bradbury 1993].

UNIVERSITY FOR INDUSTRY

The workplace is an area worthy of study and understanding, and needs to be seen as a learning environment. For this to succeed, there need to be attitude changes, so that it becomes possible for managers to admit when they do not understand, to respect the knowledge and expertise of colleagues in their organisation, and to support ongoing training and development.

Some old divisions will have to be bridged:

workers by hand	v.	workers by brain
workforce	v.	management
technology	v.	business strategy
training	v.	education

For this to succeed, those driving the new venture will need to have experience of the cultures they are seeking to unify.

Subcontracting the Management of Complexity

Modern management styles require strict adherence to deadlines, the stripping away of bureaucracy, and the clarification of the customer-supplier relationship at each stage. With the imposition of strict cash limits, little latitude is left for testing and commissioning of complex systems. Systems may go untested, with defects only emerging at the point of disastrous failure.

MONEY DOWN A HOLE

A case in point is the Channel Tunnel, where pressure from bankers left Euro-tunnel with an almost impossibly short period to test and commission new Shuttle transport systems, handicapped by a shortage of staff with practical experience and a shortage of delivered rolling stock.

The difference between "just in time" and "just too late" can be critical, affecting the overall viability of the scheme.

The Stock Exchange TAURUS system promised paperless dealings in stocks and shares. Deadlines were agreed but not adhered to, and it is hard to find senior managers who will accept responsibility for the technical failure to deliver. The work had largely been entrusted to external contractors, with limited monitoring and supervision by Stock Exchange senior staff. The new CREST system now promises better performance for a lower price.

This very complexity, and the incapacity of many organisations in the management of technical issues, provides an entry point for consultancies. Ovum seek to sell configuration management tools, arguing:

"Today's software systems are complex. With ever more power on the desktop, more and more software developers work together connected by networks. But pick up the wrong section of code over the network and the result can be anything from aircraft wings which turn out too small to the $40m lost by a bank which found out too late that there was an incorrect module in a software upgrade issued to all its branches."

"Big Bang" in the City of London in 1986 brought sudden liberalisation and deregulation to traditional financial institutions. The Financial Services Act of 1985 removed restrictions, and allowed companies to diversify into new areas of business, whether share trading, mortgages or insurance. The preparations for the change revealed a worrying reliance on the power of new technology to address problems in managing financial processes and markets that were beyond the ingenuity of individual specialists. Where the necessary expertise was not held in-house, there was a tendency to rely on the consultancy services of the major accountancy firms, now rebadged as management consultancies with large IT divisions.

GOVERNMENT AND INFORMATION TECHNOLOGY CAPABILITY

The collapse of the UK IT industry since the early 1980s has left Government in a quandary. Programmes such as Alvey were devised to develop UK capability through collaborative research and development. The major industrial partners, such as ICL and Systems Designers, have since fallen into foreign hands (Japanese and American respectively). The DTI has withdrawn from involvement in funding research and development. Government laboratories are being privately managed, and in some cases privatised. Civil Service numbers are being cut as a policy priority, leaving the major management consultancies with a captive market. Touche Ross are both managing the insolvency of the Maxwell empire and managing IKBS (intelligent knowledge-based systems) awareness programmes, despite lacking a major track record of success in either area.

RAPID REFORMS AND PRIVATISATION

High-speed privatisation and "reforms" to the National Health Service and to education services bring attendant IT disasters. Policies have been designed at speed by a group of advisers with an ideological position endorsed by Government but without practical experience of working in the fields they are seeking to transform. Ideology is to be transformed into systems to run in the real world.

Top-down management devolves responsibility for the different components of the broken-up and demoralised services, but without the necessary financial resources to enable systems to work. No thought is given to overall standards, systems and consistency: such matters are declared unimportant when market forces are left to operate.

The free operation of market forces, albeit in a wholly artificial rigged market, involves the assumption that some units may become economically unviable and collapse. As such prospects appear, the individuals concerned blame the system, or the IT elements that are visible, and IT disasters can be cited when the real issue is one of systemic disintegration.

Conversely it could be argued that centralist State control is also conducive to IT disasters. The argument is that no individual will take responsibility within a faceless State bureaucracy, and that the breakthrough comes with the introduction of market forces and private-sector disciplines.

The complication is that the private-sector model has no obvious way of addressing needs that were dealt with by the State. Where is the private-sector motivation to deal with problems of the poor in the benefits system, the special needs for telephones for the disabled, or discounted through-ticketing on public transport for the pensioner? New artificial markets have to be created, but these tend to be given low priority, waiting until the new private operators are established and applying their plans to take maximum advantage of market conditions. In the transition there is discontinuity, including the collapse of previously smooth-running systems.

Consequences of Discontinuity

The process of systems development is long, laborious and expensive. Some acceleration can be achieved by using rapid prototyping, but this cannot obviate the need for extensive usability testing. Once a system is in place, major costs are incurred through maintenance, modifications and ongoing development.

IMPOSED SYSTEMS

In recent years, and across many public and private areas of activity, the pace of policy development and change has exceeded the capacity of systems developers to respond. Wholesale changes have been implemented without pilot phases or evaluation.

In the National Health Service, the "reform" process has been under way since 1991, but with numerous changes in the relations and reporting structures between component parts. The rapid introduction of Hospital Trusts and GP Fund-holding Practices has necessitated intensive IT systems development activity, but in the absence of strategies, standards or identified budgets, other than at the expense of patient care.

In the education service, there has been constant change at all levels. Local Management of Schools, Higher Education Corporations status for Polytechnics and Colleges of Higher Education, and then Further Education Corporation status for Colleges, all have increased the requirement for IT systems. Central bodies, the Higher Education Funding Council and the Further Education Funding Council, have been given near-absolute power to determine the allocation of public funds in their sectors, but change the basis on which information is collected and analysed at least annually. It is thus not possible to develop stable systems and standards.

At the time of writing, British Rail is undergoing traumatic change, with newly introduced organisational structures cutting across previous divisional lines, and the entire change in disregard of opposition from staff and public alike. The former national system has been broken up, and nothing coherent is yet in place to replace it.

There are two alternative outcomes. For those who persist in relying on the national systems, and the results of their performance indicators and league tables, disaster is all but inevitable. There is no consistency behind the data that are processed, and no trust in the real-world sector in the conclusions derived from such processing, particularly when individuals feel themselves disadvantaged. It becomes a matter of ingenuity, finding ways of so presenting data as to defeat, or maximise outcomes from, the system.

TOOLS FOR UNDERSTANDING

A more radical alternative is to recognise the inherent limitations of IT systems in an environment of rapid change. Given that the systems are an attempted extension of the views of those who have commissioned them, there is a need for a richer understanding of the political and economic environment, and an empowerment of human decision-makers.

IT can be no more than a tool for the thinking decision-maker in an unstable world. It is not sensible to commission highly specified bespoke systems to handle the administration of an area of activity governed by legislation that is subject to frequent and unpredictable change.

Many training agents have encountered difficulties in dealing with the various schemes announced by the Department of Employment. Each involves subtle changes in rules for eligibility, structure of provision and mechanisms for funding. Each requires the development and introduction of new administrative systems, at extremely short notice. The answer has to be the empowerment of the individual to work in an IT-rich environment, where the interests of the human dominate those of the system. The exercise of human judgement and discretion is the best protection against disaster. If and when things go wrong, there is an increased likelihood that more individuals will understand the problems and what they need to do.

A Question of Scale

A fundamental principle of managing innovation, and of programming in the artificial intelligence tradition, is that we have to be able to learn from our mistakes. In programming, we learn from developing toy examples, from "programming in the small", where there are no serious adverse consequences of mistakes or "bugs" in the supported learning environment.

Our programs can only ever be imperfect models of the real-world problems with which we have to deal, but they can give us new insights and equip us to find better solutions. Similarly, a small-scale management project can provide us with insights that will serve us in later large-scale enterprises. Small-scale exercises may prove to be an inadequate preparation, in isolation, for problems with large-scale systems in an organisational context, but they have a part to play.

WE HAVE NO TECHNOLOGICAL MAGIC

Research in logic, mathematics and computer science since the 1960s has developed a body of knowledge and experience concerning reliable software. Where programs are written in languages with a foundation in mathematical logic, the programs can be considered as mathematical objects, and tested without the necessity of running in real time. Furthermore, it is possible for programs to be synthesised from their specifications in mathematical notation, and then transformed and optimised for better performance on the chosen computer system. In such cases, we can declare that the computer cannot make mistakes, for each of the stages in the transformation process is known to be correct in terms of logic and mathematics, given the data as input.

In light of such progress from the logicians and mechanical theorem-provers, it is not surprising that customers, including the US Department of Defense, have come to expect certain standards of reliability from the systems they procure. Indeed, they have proceeded to set official standards, which have to be met by software suppliers in order to secure contracts, or to secure payment for work done.

David Parnas wrote with remarkable frankness and lucidity concerning the limitations of IT when faced with complex problems [Parnas 1985]:

"In March 1983 the President asked us, as members of the scientific community, to provide the means of rendering nuclear weapons impotent and obsolete. I believe that it is our duty, as scientists and engineers, to reply that we have no technological magic that will accomplish that. The short term applied research and focused development that SDI is now funding is not going to solve the problem; the President and the public should know that."

Parnas identified a problem of public expectations: the layman, including the President of the United States, had unrealistic perceptions of the capabilities of computer systems in general:

"While most products come with an express or implied warranty, software products often carry a specific disclaimer of warranty. The lay public, familiar with only a few incidents of software failure, may regard them as exceptions caused by exceptionally inept programmers. Those of us who are software professionals know better, the most competent programmers in the world cannot avoid such problems."

It is easy for Governments, or company Boards, to require that formal methods be used as the basis of new systems. Such stipulations give them a clear conscience when commissioning work. The computer science community has found it impossible to meet such standards: it is made up of fallible humans, competing for contracts in the market-place, and without the support of a professional structure and ladder of qualifications.

Given the speed of development of computer technology, it is perhaps unsurprising that the profession of computer science was poorly developed. Parnas pointed to the immaturity and fallibility of software engineering by comparison with other engineering disciplines:

"Worsening the difference between software and other areas of technology is a personnel problem. Most designers in traditional engineering disciplines have been educated to understand the mathematical tools that are available to them. Most programmers cannot even begin to use the meagre tools that are available to software engineers."

It may be misleading, in fact, to talk of computer science. The practice of computer science is normally far from scientific. According to Parnas:

"Programming is a trial and error craft. People write programs without any expectation that they will be right the first time. They spend at least as much time testing them and correcting errors as they spent writing the initial program. Programmers cannot be trusted to test their own programs adequately. Software is released for use, not when it is known to be correct, but when the rate of discovering new errors slows down to one that management considers acceptable. Users learn to accept errors and are often told how to avoid the bugs until the problem is improved."

When you hire a consultant to work on a software project, you cannot assume a long professional track record and a sequence of academic courses of study. The real world of computing and IT has grown at such an explosive speed, and people have been judged by apparent results. Software developers will often hand over a system and evade involvement in ongoing maintenance and support, so that the limitations of their work only appear after they are beyond call.

A QUESTION OF TRUST

Parnas wrote in less-technical terms about the Strategic Defense Initiative in the *New York Times* for 12th July 1985:

"Because of the extreme demands on the system and our inability to trust it, we will never be able to believe, with any confidence, that we have succeeded. Most of the money spent will be wasted."

His stand was courageous, and was seen by many of his colleagues as heretical. Parnas was not only turning down lucrative research and consultancy funding from a reputable source, but he was casting aspersions on the professional and moral credentials of those who acted otherwise.

He summed the matter up in a manner that was more general, and which relates to the complexity and criticality of the project:

"The worst thing is that we wouldn't trust the system if we did build it."

If we could not trust such systems, could we trust those who were prepared to build them? What do computer science professionals have to know in order to be worthy of our confidence?

EDUCATING SOFTWARE ENGINEERS

The key to the problem is clearly education, both of computer science professionals and of those who commission their work. In a new Renaissance Age, we could imagine IT specialists who understood management, and managers who understood IT. We are still in the Dark Ages.

Considering issues of professional education Parnas [1990] wrote:

"Certification is intended to protect public safety by making certain that engineers have a solid grounding in fundamental science and mathematics, are aware of their professional responsibilities, and are trained to be thorough and complete in their analysis." (p. 17)

His argument was again broader than defence projects, but raises critical questions about the builders of complex systems:

"Where a scientist may be happy with a device that validates his theory, an engineer is taught to make sure that the device is efficient, reliable, safe, easy to use, and robust." (p. 17)

Questions arise about the professionalism of software engineers:

"As engineers in other fields are becoming more dependent on computing devices in their own professional practice, they are also becoming more concerned about the lack of professionalism in the products they use." (p. 19)

This in turn suggests a need for changes in the education of such professionals:

"Graduates need the fundamentals that will allow a lifetime of learning new developments." (p. 22)

Similar concerns were expressed by a group convened by the British Computer Society and Institute for Electrical Engineers, in their consideration of curricula for software engineering [BCS/IEE 1989]:

"Although software products do not degrade, human intervention may degrade them. They depend on the environment and cannot without renewed tests of fitness for purpose be transferred to environments other than those for which they were designed." (p. 12)

They expressed worry about the backgrounds of many of those who produce software, and the consequent limitations of their products:

"The software produced by people whose principal skill is in another discipline is often a prototype, suitable for demonstrating feasibility, but unsuited to production and sustained use." (p. 13)

As practitioners working with a rapidly changing technology, theoretical understanding is vital:

"Some of the intellectual tools and methods of software engineering are at present skills in process of development, and rapid change is to be expected for some time to come. Software engineers therefore need the theoretical understanding which will be a foundation for learning and using new methods in the future, and the cast of mind which sees the constant updating of knowledge as required professional behaviour." (p. 14)

Working on Infeasible Projects

Professor Manny Lehman was Head of the influential Department of Computing at Imperial College at the time of the Strategic Defense Initiative, and chaired a panel discussion, to which David Parnas contributed, at a software engineering conference in 1985. He subsequently wrote [Lehman 1985] to his colleagues to explain his decision to accept consultancy work on SDI. Lehman argued that he was entitled to concentrate solely on technical issues, ignoring any consequences of the project going ahead:

> "*I believe that I am qualified and informed to judge on technical issues relating to SDI software, but not sufficiently well-informed to judge, for example, related political, strategic or legal aspects. I do not, in general, trust politicians of any ilk and from any country in terms of their public utterances and do not regard their publicly expressed views as accurate or as a basis for decision making. Thus I cannot, for example, judge whether a US commitment to SDI increases or decreases the chances of nuclear catastrophe, either could be the case.*"

The mere fact that the project was clearly technically infeasible should not prevent him from working on it:

> "*Provided one has clearly stated that project objectives, as stated, appear unachievable, and provided one can identify alternative goals for the work to be undertaken, for example clarifying what can and what cannot be done and why, there seems to be no moral problem of this type, in involvement.*"

SOFTWARE POLLUTION

Lehman identified a number of potential benefits from working on SDI. He was concerned above all with combating what he termed "software pollution":

> "*The problem of developing software technology that overcomes the threat of software pollution is an urgent one. SDI is an extreme example of the challenges that face system and software designers everywhere; a unique development environment for software technology, its methods, tools and techniques. Working and exploration within that environment should rapidly advance the technology and provide the society with the means to better control the current indiscriminate use of computers; to ensure their exploitation in a manner that will benefit, not destroy, mankind and its way of life. Reduction of the threat of software pollution is an urgent necessity.*"

Only scientific and technical specialists could be qualified to argue that the system was not feasible, and the only way in which the case could be made was from within the programme. There was, therefore, no alternative to participation:

> "*We who know that the system is not feasible, that the claims are incorrect and that, therefore, any benefit stems from side effects, have the duty to demonstrate scientific and technological reasons for our views; the intrinsic nature of the problem that makes it about as unrealistic as a project to build a projectile whose speed exceeds the speed of light. Only activity from within can develop a technically convincing case, letters to the press or to politicians, however well intentioned, are simply treated by decision makers as emotional or politically triggered reactions.*"

Although Lehman argued in favour of participation by scientists in SDI, he saw the greatest danger as being posed by computer systems themselves:

"In a sense software pollution represents a threat to mankind greater than that from nuclear weapons, if only because defence mechanisms are based on software and because military and government information analysis on which policy and strategy are based is increasingly using computer based systems to support them in their intelligence analysis."

The Case for Programming

The concerns expressed by Parnas and Lehman have serious implications for general managers, who depend on the effective working of software and software engineers. It is too easy for managers simply to "require" that all systems work first time, every time.

There is a strong case for giving all managers some experience of programming, with the objective, not of becoming professional programmers, but of understanding something of the potential and limitations of information systems, and indeed of all systems. Managers benefit from practical experience of a culture that they may have to manage, and with which they may have to communicate at times of stress. Such experience may reduce the dangers of disaster arising from crises, as it may serve to break down cultural barriers within the organisation.

The suggestion that managers should be exposed to programming can provoke hostility, as it is variously argued that:

- Programming is no longer required with advanced systems.
- Technical matters should be left to technicians.
- Managers should remain detached from operational details.
- Specialist programming skills can be bought-in when required.

IS PROGRAMMING DEAD?

All managers now tend to want computers on their desks, and to have access to management information, seen as central to the financial monitoring and control that is a key part of their job. Formerly they might have been concerned with access to a corporate decision support system or executive information system; now they want to make use of the standard business software available to them as individuals or on the corporate network. As they develop macros in a spreadsheet or database, they are engaged in programming, though not in a traditional computer language. By manipulating commercial packages, they may

be protected from the underlying models that form the basis of both the management problem and the software solution. When packages change, or when links
are required between separate systems, subject and technical understanding is
needed.

SHOULD TECHNICAL MATTERS BE LEFT FOR TECHNICIANS?

To leave such matters to technicians may be dangerous if they lack the understanding of and responsibility for the business problem for which a solution is
being sought. Managers abdicate control of their own areas of responsibility if
they become fully dependent on the advice and knowledge of others whose
priorities and objectives may be different. For example, the technician will have
had particular past experience with languages and systems, which influence his
judgements and recommendations. He may have a favoured technological
solution for which he is seeking matching business problems.

SHOULD MANAGERS BE DETACHED FROM OPERATIONAL DETAILS?

The separation of strategic and operational levels may be seen as problematic in
the area of IT, when strategic vision must be tempered by what is operationally
possible. Managers who remain aloof from technology may find their services
are seen as superfluous when downsizing and delayering take place.

CAN WE BUY-IN SPECIALIST PROGRAMMING SKILLS?

Business development may be impeded by the absence of local skills in the areas
required. If the decision is made to buy-in consultancy as and when necessary,
this presumes the availability of appropriate affordable expertise. It also assumes
that technical resources can be thrown at a business problem without specialist
domain understanding. Somebody needs to have the expertise to make that
judgement.

Issues of Integration

4

We are not interested in the possibilities of defeat; they do not exist.

Queen Victoria (1819–1901)

Managing IT in the Organisation

Information technology is now all-pervasive; it may be managed, but it cannot be controlled. As managers increasingly have access to the same technology at home as at work, there can be conflicts between individual and organisational modes of use.

PC SECURITY

PCs made it into most organisations by stealth. Since they owe their presence to a breach of vigilance, and a wide assortment of budgets, it is hardly surprising that most PC users put security low on their list of priorities. Many PCs are purchased and administered by end-users who think they are doing well if they remember to back up their data once a month.

Things are often no better at mainframe installations, which have full-time security officers and security policies. Too often, these professionals forget about PC security altogether. PCs are no longer stand-alone, personal productivity tools; the majority are networked and many double up as terminals connected to the mainframe. If you fail to secure them, then the back door to the corporate database is wide open.

According to a recent DTI/NCC survey, 832 companies suffered 1029 virus attacks in two years, at an estimated cost of £4000 a time.

Good computer security is an attitude of mind; the more so on PCs, since that may be the only influence the security professionals have over an amateur, although largely autonomous, user base. These people need training and advice, and it is up to the IT professionals to make sure they get it, with the support of line managers across the organisation.

OUTSOURCING

Given the complexity of managing IT with limited budgets, limited technical expertise and an absence of support from Board level, it is hardly surprising that in many organisations the decision has been made to pass the problem on to others, and to establish outsourcing arrangements.

At the launch of any new outsourcing deal, sugar-coated phrases from both parties tend to abound:

- Advantageous alliance
- Strategic partnership
- Use of specialist skills
- Pooling of resources
- Shared benefits

Recent experience of outsourcing suggests a different tone: "Always expect the worst, and plan for it" ["A business guide to outsourcing", *Business Intelligence* 1994]. This guide reported on the outsourcing experience of 160 major European companies. It estimated that the British outsourcing market was worth about £800 million in 1993. Just over half of UK respondents were outsourcing IT.

About 70% of users who have outsourced have met with problems and half of them have had formal disputes with vendors. Businesses reported outsourcing relationships that were plagued by inflexible contracts, vendors who would not collaborate, costs spiralling out of control and ill-defined service levels.

Measuring the realistic savings from outsourcing, before taking the decision to outsource, is imperative. In 1988, a vendor approached the BBC, promising savings of 40%. The BBC's own analysis concluded that there would only be 10% savings.

One in 20 companies interviewed were planning to bring their IT back in-house by 1994. If users need expertise in deciding their IT direction, they should consider embarking on "insourcing deals", which would bring in project managers or business analysts.

The report predicts that growth in outsourcing in the UK will be "patchy": 20% in central Government, 12% in local government and 6% in the private sector.

Some in those sectors will reap the benefits of outsourcing: value for money, flexibility, access to technology, freeing financial capital. Others may encounter problems because they failed to specify service levels, failed to cover all issues in the contract, changed their requirements, and experienced unforeseen charges. We can expect controversies over outsourcing to rival those over personal pensions and life insurance, where unscrupulous agents are accused of negotiating deals that maximised their individual commission earnings.

Loss of control of the strategic use of IT was a problem:

"You cannot outsource outsourcing. You can outsource a great deal of the doing of the service, but not the responsibility for it."

"Outsourcing is not about saving a few bob on the IT in the short term, it is about long-term commitment."

From the perspective of corporate strategy, to the extent that IT is critical for the future of the organisation, it could be fatal for control of the IT function to fall into the hands of others.

PRESSURES ON CHIEF INFORMATION OFFICERS

The problem with a specific job title is that the holder is then expected to perform the specific job, even if the necessary resources and decision-making power are not available.

Deloitte and Touche surveyed 400 chief information officers. The survey indicated that budgets only increased 0.4% in 1993, while the consumer price index rose 2.7%. At the same time, CIOs were expected to lead the charge towards re-engineering their businesses and moving critical applications onto client–server architectures.

Information systems managers have to implement new applications in some form of client–server mode, and cannot even consider buying another mainframe. Client–server is taken to mean making better use of PCs, and delivering information through a graphical user interface.

According to the survey, the CIOs believe that 60% of their mission-critical applications need to be improved radically. Getting more of them to client–server mode is part of the answer.

As many as 43% of CIOs named high implementation costs and lack of industry standards as major barriers to implementing client–server, while the main issue, cited by 54%, was a lack of qualified personnel.

The combination of tight budgets, pressure to move to client–server and lack of qualified personnel add up to a high degree of risk for CIOs.

SECURITY RISKS WITH GROUPWARE

Vendors of new software products would have customers believe that they are providing the solution to major management problems. Unless there are major advances in security systems and staff training, groupware has the potential to cause distributed disasters.

The ease with which a network operator accidentally disabled an international Notes network in April 1994 emphasises the need to have server security, and a usage policy for distributed environments.

Arthur Andersen, which relies heavily on the Lotus Notes groupware product, suddenly lost the use of its Notes net because of a network operator's error. The employee was developing a new application, and inadvertently wiped out much of a user directory on the server on which he was working.

Notes' replication feature, usually one of its advantages, ensured that Arthur Andersen's shrunken user directory was quickly distributed to hundreds of servers on the company's 30 000-user Notes network.

The next day, many Arthur Andersen employees were unable to use the network, a problem minimised by the fact that the replication occurred on Friday night and Saturday morning. Arthur Andersen was also helped by a policy of backing up servers routinely.

HELPDESKS

The spread of IT use has necessitated the development of a new group of professionals, manning helpdesks. They serve as the "emergency service" of the organisation, providing calm support for executives whose electronic world appears to have fallen apart.

Users give little thought to helpdesks until that awful day when the screen goes blank or the keyboard seizes up.

Dr Petra Burgisser, of Hoffman-La Roche, is responsible for their central help-desk facility. With 1500 to 2000 calls a month, the helpdesk has had to regulate every aspect of its work. Each call, for example, is assigned a priority. It aims to resolve 80% of priority-one calls, where users cannot work, in less than 10 minutes, and 100% in less than a day. Of priority-two calls, where users are prevented from getting on with their work, 80% should be answered in less than a day, and all in under two weeks. Priority-three calls are where a problem exists, but users are unaffected – 95% of these should be solved in less than three weeks.

Helpdesk operations cannot work in isolation, but must be integrated with other service functions. Equally important is laying down defined rules for managing problems and their hand-over to the various technical service groups looking after areas such as networking or e-mail.

Helpdesk staff have to work with both very technologically sophisticated and unsophisticated people. At one moment they are speaking to customers, who frequently do not understand half the technology terms; and at the next to the highly skilled technicians who can solve the problem. Above all there has to be a focus on customers. They want access to a knowledgeable person who can solve the problem, a quick solution, people who are sensitive to the impact of the problem on their particular business, and people who both take time to understand and have the tenacity to pursue it.

A STRATEGIC APPROACH

The accountants and management consultants Price Waterhouse maintained, in their International Review of 1990:

> *"Tight cost controls combined with improved price/performance ratios look like squeezing hardware budgets in some countries. After a boom in software expenditure, indications are that this area is also coming under close scrutiny. Management continues to increase its use of outsourcing, in reply to the shortage of skilled staff. Unbridled growth in decentralisation of computing power to the users at last shows signs of being brought under control. The number one worry of computer executives is now the integration of IT with company objectives, as business concerns take precedence over technical issues."*

We can detect an impatience with technical detail, and a determination to control costs, typically obliging the IT function to report to the Finance Director.

In their IT Review of 1990–91, Price Waterhouse presented a dramatic and simplified view of the role of IT in strategic management:

> *"IT is data processing*
> *automation*
> *communication*
> *recording*
> *knowledge*
> *artificial intelligence*
> *Yesterday it was about managing experts.*
> *Today it is the very stuff of management.*
> *Tomorrow there may be little else that needs to be managed."*

On this argument, outsourcing the IT leaves strategic managers with little to do, and with little control over their own destinies. Within the organisation, they see pressure to reduce expenditure on IT.

Since about 1984 we have seen reduced corporate expenditure on IT, as top management has challenged IT budgets, not daunted by technical arguments. Given that the price of money has been high, the justification for investment has been harder to make. Furthermore, although the price of computers is falling, replacement of old systems could involve full rewriting of critical systems. The tendency has been to make do and mend.

Many organisations have moved to internal charging systems, attributing costs for centrally provided services. Price Waterhouse see this as a divisive approach:

> *"Charging the users for costs they can't control is divisive."*

As a literature grows concerned with the use of IT for competitive advantage, we can discern the development of a backlash, from managers reluctant to assign a privileged position to IT as against other functions:

"Why should a methodology exist for achieving competitive advantage with IT, and for no other area of business?"

Price Waterhouse are properly sceptical about the prospects for technically driven security systems. Organisations face a collective challenge, and "managing security is about learning to live with the problem". They advise against undue reliance on ingenious solutions, presented as foolproof:

"Anything a human being can put up, another can pull down."

"The whole exercise is about getting the staff security conscious."

For all the demonising of outside threats, greater dangers come from within the organisation:

"The amount of damage caused by hackers and viruses has, to date, been considerably less than users do to themselves accidentally every day. Their importance is the way they have highlighted the potential vulnerability of an IT based business, and an IT based society. Since we cannot remove this, we must learn to live with it ... the only effective approach is the education of users."

MORE BUSINESS FOR ACCOUNTANTS AND CONSULTANTS

The point of these reports is, of course, to secure additional business. In their report on European IT services, Price Waterhouse declared that:

"Developing and implementing a successful system demands a total understanding of the business functions it is to serve and the current best practice."

As accountants and management consultants, they now present themselves as experts in the management of IT:

"Ensuring effective communication demands close attention and probably calls for major investment too. It is a major source of data capture and data dissemination, and requires specialists to create a cost-effective system that fulfils all your needs."

There is the assumption that outside specialists, such as their staff, are needed:

"To assess the performance of an IT system, you must be able to measure its impact on your company's performance, for the price you are paying. The techniques that ensure that you are using IT cost-effectively are essential."

Who better than accountants to advise on cost-effectiveness?

"And then there are the risk factors. Is there a weak link in your data security? Will your disaster recovery programme really stand the apocalyptic challenge of fire and flood?"

There is no real answer to that, but the client begins to worry:

"Would you paint your own masterpiece if you had a Leonardo to call on?"

It all depends on whether the act of painting is seen as worth while in itself; will someone else's disaster recovery plan do the job?

UNDERSTANDING TECHNOLOGY AND ORGANISATIONS

In contrast, Bessant and Rothwell [1992] argue for a wider view of technology, encompassing knowledge and skill. Their analysis is of fifth-wave organisations, making integrated use of intelligent technologies. Rather than thinking in the simple terms of competitive advantage, they look at a more knowledge-based approach:

"A key feature of this fifth wave is the re-emphasis on technology as a total system, involving not only tools and equipment but also the knowledge and skill with which to use them, and the ways in which their use is planned, controlled and organised to serve the purpose of the enterprise." (p. 192)

On this account IT cannot be floated off as a separate function for distinct treatment:

"Managing innovation within this context becomes a matter of understanding the complex web of interconnections which make for success, and recognising the intangible and ephemeral character of many of these." (p. 194)

Blackler and Brown [1985] noted that the introduction of new systems was rarely considered when such systems were designed and justified. They published their critique at the time of the British Government's Alvey Programme in Advanced Information Technology, which was very much technology-driven, with limited involvement from users, and little discussion of IT strategy issues:

"We came across no examples where a prime concern of systematic evaluation has been the manner in which the new systems have been designed and introduced." (p. 1)

Given the prevailing assumptions that new technologies implied progress, justifications were cursory:

"If there is any chance of justifying the new systems in a conventional way then this tends to be attempted (even though optimistic or unrealistic promises may be necessitated e.g. staff savings on word processors). Only where this is not feasible does it seem that value added/organisational benefits tend to be highlighted. In the absence of relevant corporate guidelines, this may involve relatively junior staff making what may be thought to be uncomfortable references to broad corporate strategies."

It is in such organisations that we can now expect to find decisions to outsource.

HUMAN NETWORKING

Blanning [1987] saw managers as significant players in the information game:

"Managers are increasingly being viewed as participants in a network of shared information, opinions and advice. This view supplements the traditional views of managers as leaders, decision makers, organisation developers etc. and it suggests that an important purpose of a DSS is to help managers to participate in networks of human and computerised information sources."

Human networking skills are vital, requiring the manager to go beyond the normal reporting channels:

"Successful managers develop a network of information sources both inside and outside of their organisations, and many of the inside sources are outside of the manager's chain of command. The purpose of the network is to help the manager to obtain and verify information relevant to immediate or future decisions, to convince others of the propriety of these decisions, to monitor the progress of implementation, and to enhance the network for possible future use."

Collins [1987] has emphasised the importance of skill and tacit knowledge, underlying systems in use:

"The design of crafted artefacts is design for open systems use and is not an exact science: in addition to formal theories, principles of design rest on traditional ways of doing things, on artisan's skills and on bodies of tacit knowledge that cannot be fully articulated."

Systems have to be seen in their cultural context, and as inseparable from the end-user:

"A machine cannot be understood aside from its end-user and the cultural ambience in which it works. The role of the end-user is to insert that part of the iceberg of cultural knowledge that cannot be programmed."

Expert Systems and Mainstream Software

Two nations; between whom there is no intercourse and no sympathy; who are as ignorant of each other's habits, thoughts and feelings, as if they were dwellers in different zones, or inhabitants of different planets; who are formed by a different breeding, are fed by a different food, are ordered by different manners, and are not governed by the same laws.

Benjamin Disraeli (1804–81), Sybil, 1845

In Britain we can see a cultural separation between the intellectuals of the artificial intelligence community, and the pragmatics of business and mainstream computer science. Communication and understanding across the divide has been limited. The potential for benefits is great, with critical criteria applied by both sides. Indeed, collaborative technical advance accompanied by scepticism is a promising approach to preventing IT disasters.

BRITISH SCEPTICISM

Max Bramer was one of the founding members of the British Computer Society Expert Systems Group, but has provided a series of cautionary warnings over the years [Bramer 1985]:

"The most negative aspect of the developments of the last few years is probably that of expectations raised unrealistically high."

Following a period of publicised research, companies have been reluctant to accept that technical problems might remain:

"The theoretical problems involved in developing Artificial Intelligence systems have not suddenly ceased to exist, simply because it may sometimes be inconvenient to recognise them."

Bramer [1987] tried to alert the computing community to the slenderness of the technical base on which their future plans are predicated:

"Although there are individuals and research groups considering such theoretical and methodological matters, the need for a satisfactory methodology for all aspects of the development and maintenance of Expert Systems, and the importance of placing consistency maintenance, reasoning with uncertainty etc. on a sound theoretical basis seems little appreciated by most of those developing systems 'in the field', as indeed was the need for properly founded development methodologies for conventional Data Processing systems not long ago."

Partridge [1986] has drawn attention to the different assumptions and technical foundations underlying artificial intelligence as opposed to conventional software, and argues that "AI as practical software is not just about to happen". He cites two main reasons:

"1.   The research-based incremental AI program development paradigm does not produce programs that exhibit the necessary characteristics of practical software: comprehensibility, reliability, robustness, and maintainability.

2.   AI programs are not correct or incorrect; they are, at best, adequate. Adequacy is a complex, context-dependent quality that can be maintained in a variety of different contexts only by means of a sophisticated self-modifying capability (machine learning). The problems of self-adaptive programs are AI research topics, they are not ready for inclusion in practical software."

As Gillies [1991] argues, the world of computer science has long been divided into the two cultures of software engineering and artificial intelligence. The gap was narrowed by the development of commercial expert systems, and by the increased availability of powerful tools on affordable hardware. In recent years the working products of artificial intelligence laboratory research have been absorbed into computer science, but methodological differences remain.

Gillies gives clear examples of the integration of the strengths of expert systems prototyping with software development methodologies and the formal requirements of software engineering. The "missing link" has frequently been the use of PROLOG, which derives from artificial intelligence but has proved an efficient and reliable prototyping tool for those who understand its limitations. With current concerns for quality and quality assurance, Gillies draws attention to the inherent limitations of knowledge-based systems, and addresses the requirements of official standards.

AMERICAN TECHNOLOGICAL OPTIMISM

In contrast, American texts [e.g. Giarratano and Riley 1989] radiate technological optimism. NASA scientists take an extreme view of the future of their country – "automate, emigrate or evaporate" – and see their CLIPS system as "an important step in the evolution of a technology that may be the most important advance in the history of mankind". Such books exude the technological optimism that so pervades Disneyworld and its Cape Canaveral annexe.

More pragmatically, Dan Shafer argues [Shafer 1990]:

"Artificial Intelligence, to be successful, is going to have to disappear. Only when it is invisibly embedded into everyday software will AI achieve anything resembling commercial acceptance."

Shafer offers a practical cookbook, enabling business users of personal computers to build front-ends to spreadsheets and databases using tools such as KnowledgePro and VP-Expert, healthily demystifying advanced technology. The same hardware will now support the transition to advanced software concepts, motivated by business needs. In a world where computers are typically only used to a fraction of their potential, such an approach is welcome.

In Harmon and Sawyer [1990] Ed Feigenbaum reminds us of the expert systems revolution, its implications for productivity, and the importance of planning by managers and Governments. He notes that the US Government "eschews national planning for information technology outside of the defense context". The new information superhighway, making civil use of previously defence-oriented network systems, may represent a major step forward.

Harmon and Sawyer [1990] proclaim the good news of knowledge engineering, while warning of the difficulties of knowledge acquisition. This is not simply a technical bottleneck to be removed by new techniques. We are coming to understand the limitations of our attempts to formalise knowledge.

KNOWLEDGE MANAGEMENT

Karl Wiig addressed a European context of users of personal computers, and gave due attention to personnel and project management issues [Wiig 1990]. Rather than offering expert systems as a quick fix, he highlighted the risks as well as the benefits, and urged the importance of a thorough knowledge of the business for which the system is being constructed. Domain expertise and management skill have previously been underrated in the concentration on technology.

Wiig reflected on the importance of knowledge management:

"The focus of knowledge management is to harness and control the organisation's expertise to preserve it and to put it to use in the best possible ways."

The DTI "Manufacturing Intelligence" programme [DTI 1991] has sought to address the problem of risks from poorly understood systems based on artificial intelligence and expert systems. When asked whether there is a danger of the system going "berserk", the answer is hedged with caution:

"Not if it is developed properly, and the area of operation is fully understood. However, the output from the system can be no better than the information provided. If the system contains ambiguous or incomplete rules, or applies to processes which are not fully understood, it can serve only as an advisor to an untrained operator, and a skilled person may still be required."

It would be a brave person who could claim that their rules were unambiguous, complete, and applied to processes that are fully understood. Alternatively, we are considering only small application areas. Ambitions have become more properly modest. Training, apprenticeships and procedure manuals can now be joined by expert systems development in meeting this need.

From a more academic, but transatlantic, standpoint, Partridge and Wilks [1990] bring together valuable sources. Commercial success and popularisation have obscured the continuing fundamental debates among AI researchers.

- Are AI programs distinct from other parts of computer science?
- Can there be experiments in AI, or is it rather an engineering discipline?
- Is the methodology of AI different from that of software engineering?
- Does logic programming provide the answer to all our problems?
- Does AI have to model some aspect of human processing?
- What is the status of neural networks?

It is important for managers to have some understanding of these questions, and of the range of answers available.

In a classic reference text from Stanford [Barr *et al.* 1990] there is an increased emphasis on issues, principles and theory, rather than simple accounts of particular systems. As the introduction says:

"It reflects a significant maturation of AI that this volume of the Handbook is less concerned with the systems we build than with what we have learned and have still to learn by building them."

The themes are "blackboard systems", "cooperative distributed problem solving", "expert systems", "natural language understanding", "qualitative physics", "knowledge-based simulation" and "computer vision". Each has potential long-term implications for business.

Kurzweil [1990] is perhaps best known as the developer of the world's first print-to-speech reading machine for the blind and the voice-activated word processor. He sees artificial intelligence in the human context. Despite the benevolent applications for the disabled, he notes that:

"Computer technology is already a powerful ally of the totalitarian."

Post-industrial society, he argues:

"... will be fuelled not by oil but by a new commodity called Artificial Intelligence."

He emphasises the importance of education:

"A lesson we can draw ... is the importance of education and training in a world relying increasingly on skill and innovation and decreasingly on material resources."

EXPECTATIONS

Commercial consultants, such as in Beerel [1993], have come to assume the maturity of the commercial field. They omit to mention the University research background, or fundamental research issues that remain to be addressed. The technical framework is taken as given, with further insights available through consultancy such as offered by the author. Systems development methodologies are cited in passing, but without references or serious analysis of fundamental assumptions. It is assumed that expert systems shells, implemented on personal computers, provide the appropriate base for system development, and that there is a central role for the consultant knowledge engineer. Beerel's initial frank account of prototyping an expert system for a client is somewhat worrying; her consultancy agreed to produce a prototype credit advisory system within weeks of meeting the client, despite a lack of prior technical background.

We have yet to be told of the disaster stories, where automated loan evaluation may have contributed to the 1980s boom and 1990s slump. The truth behind the technology of "Big Bang" and financial deregulation may remain "commercial in confidence" to protect the guilty.

The existence of some success stories gives us insights into potential disasters. The London-based International Futures Exchange (LIFFE) demonstrates the viability of modern electronic trading, supported by rigorous self-regulation, state-of-the-art technology, and confidence in the probity of management. LIFFE has been fortunate in the timing of its establishment and development; the Stock Exchange and Lloyds Insurance Market have many lessons to learn.

There has been little discussion of the limits of expert systems, and problems of integration with disparate systems in a business and real-time situation. The recommended approach of hiring consultants as and when required may protect an organisation from considering its own problems, and from appreciating local expertise in the knowledge domain.

There has been little attention given to the critical issues of tacit knowledge and human-centred systems. Rule-based systems may be used to represent a proportion of the propositional knowledge of the expert or experienced practitioner, but real expertise involves going beyond the rules, using tacit knowledge of how things are and how things are done which may be held as part of the culture. Problem-solving is all too often seen from the perspective of the individual top-down manager, rather than as a group concern, involving collaboration and cooperation.

Management and Information Systems

The battle rages to establish the foundations of this critical field. As Wysocki and Young [1990] say:

> *"Although realigning Information Systems production and management processes depends heavily on the 'tribal knowledge' of experienced and battle-scarred IS managers, no broad scientific tradition of IS management reflecting such cumulative knowledge has evolved or at least has not been well published. There is as yet no reliable road map for up-and-coming IS managers to follow."*

They place their emphasis on management, rather than technological tricks. They write from an American context, while in a less technology-rich Britain the debate on hybrid management has had a different emphasis, seeking to add some technological awareness to the general manager who has delegated information systems responsibilities to others.

Ward *et al.* [1990] argue that:

> *"Information Systems are more appropriately conceived as social systems which rely, to a greater and lesser extent, on new technology for their operation."*

They consider investment in information systems, and concentrate on strategic planning. They adopt the approach of portfolio management, and consider the "supply" management strategies that can bring together the means by which the plans are to be achieved.

THE FADING APPEAL OF INFORMATION TECHNOLOGY

Kit Grindley of Price Waterhouse gives a down-to-earth account of IT management, identifying a time in the 1980s when IT lost its allure to finance directors [Grindley 1991]:

"The management of IT at board level is either the short-term role of taking the mystique out of computing, and managing the difficult task of splitting up the existing centralised IT department by distributing its functions amongst the users; or the long-term role of building communications infrastructures, information storage infrastructure and data capture and data processing infrastructures, to support and integrate the do-it-yourself user movement."

IT management has not been as rigorous as that of other functional areas. Either insufficient effort has been devoted to traditional business planning or control methods do not work in this new area. Grindley argues that the key issues are not technical, but human:

"The important issues are human issues: of enthusiasm, or attempted pragmatism, of skills and fears, of retraining and rethinking. They are management issues: of planning and control in a new world ... where our once-trusted rulers no longer seem to measure correctly."

Open and Distributed Systems

The world of computing in business has changed at breakneck speed, and we can be sure that change will continue. The days of the mainframe and computer centre have gone, and successful management of (or with) information technology depends on an understanding of networks, client–server systems, distributed applications and open systems. It is no longer possible to delegate such matters to others, as every manager is a user of IT, and under pressure to derive competitive advantage from every keystroke. The culture of British management has traditionally been militantly non-technical and anti-academic, presenting some challenges for those who seek industrial survival. A literature is emerging, targeted on the non-specialist manager.

OPEN SYSTEMS

As Hugo [1993] points out, the British Government declined to define "Open Systems" even when launching an initiative in the field: successful role models are hard to find. Hugo's conclusion is worthy of consideration:

"Cooperation, trust, and the willingness to work together to establish and maintain effective systems are the best way to meet the objectives of both sides."

Open Systems depends for its success on open working relations. There are no easy answers, no instant panaceas. Managers have to be prepared to learn, and to take advice from unfamiliar quarters. Traditional top-down management styles are anachronistic when the technology supports distributed processing and horizontal networking. Managers who do not learn how to be part of the new solution will form part of the problem.

In the age of Open Systems, it would be easy to imagine that problems of compatibility, whether in hardware or software, were a thing of the past. Expectations of smooth-running integrated systems have been raised, so reports of difficulties in particular cases tend to meet an unsympathetic audience. British Rail have had similar problems in the cases of snow and leaves, which can be of the "wrong kind".

Built into the design of computer systems is the assumption that the users will need to upgrade their technology, probably at regular intervals. Each component purchased comes with a hidden cost in terms of built-in obsolescence and consequent additional purchases.

Over time *de facto* standards develop, and as they in turn undergo standardisation on a wide scale, a set of core elements is defined as standard, while further elements may vary within specified parameters. To update existing systems to meet developing standards may prove to be more expensive than starting afresh, but it may be required in order to provide an upgrade path for software applications and corporate databases.

The key issues are frequently communications and transportability:

- Can data from one system be used on another?
- Can a word-processed document from one proprietary package be enhanced using another?
- Can two different boxes communicate via a common network?

Cultures can develop within user communities (often poorly documented, if at all), which inhibit or prevent exchanges between groups. The incompatibility that causes greatest difficulties is at the level not of hardware or software, but of people.

Open Systems should improve disaster recovery. Open Systems defines standard interfaces and should increase the organisation's options should disaster strike. Applications and databases could be transferred to any suitable platform, while communication services could be re-established by a variety of means.

DISTRIBUTED SYSTEMS

Open Systems also enables distributed processing to be developed. Distributed applications are inherently more resilient to hardware failure than large mainframes simply because hardware resources are distributed and risk of failure is spread over a number of components. Distributed systems can be planned with added redundancy, spread over a number of processors, to cater for likely failures without resorting to the need for a complete hot standby, with the associated costs that this involves.

This does not mean that you can avoid thinking about disaster planning. For example, application source code still needs to be lodged in safe custody and you need to ensure that procedures exist for taking regular database backups.

Open Systems should be more secure. Open Systems allows flexibility and enables the free flow of information between authorised users, However, this does not mean that it is less secure than a proprietary systems approach.

Security provision should form part of IT systems irrespective of whether they are based on proprietary or Open Systems standards. Both are subject to exactly the same security risks and hazards and both should be given appropriate protection. Security is also much more than secure communications or password access. All security aspects such as physical, personnel, technical and organisa-tional security should be re-examined in planning a major review of IT struc-tures as part of an investigation of Open Systems or, indeed, proprietary systems.

Sun Microsystems have pioneered the development of Open Systems, but the majority of their experience has been gained in the scientific and technical research markets, rather than with non-specialist business managers. Systems may not be perceived as very open or friendly if they turn out to require expertise in Unix in order to achieve success.

Business Health

It has become popular to apply medical language to the consideration of software project management, with talk of "sick projects", which may, coincidentally, be based in "sick buildings". Project managers do not usually start with a "green-field site", but have to deal with existing organisational structures and post-holders, and face the challenge of recovery of ailing software projects. Whatever the internal problems, the external demands continue:

"The customer may not always be right, but the customer is always ... the customer."

There can be a critical tension between the flow of information that is required for ideas to develop, and the pressures of commercial confidentiality. Pro-fessionals may be under great pressure to withhold sensitive information, on the grounds of commercial confidentiality.

It is a matter of fine judgement how policies of computer security should be applied. In areas such as health care, cooperation and information sharing might be considered more appropriate than all-out competition and the application of market forces, leading to restrictions on information flows.

Where a system performs an irreplaceable function for the organisation, there may be an overwhelming case for redundancy, for operating spare capacity that can be switched-in in times of trouble, for a "spare-parts surgery" approach to system design and maintenance, and for intensive-care facilities to be available on constant standby.

IT health care does not come cheap, but may be seen as essential for saving corporate lives. Collective provision of services for a group of subscribers of itself imposes standards on the conduct of individual organisations and their users, with consequential reductions in freedom of decision-making.

Computer Viruses

Computer viruses have caused considerable concern in the popular press, and plagued the lives of computer users, but have received insufficient attention from senior managers, who have been slow to recognise that the corruption of computer software can lead to corporate disasters from which recovery may not be possible. Given that panic is bad for morale, it has been easier to delegate responsibility and carry on regardless.

IMPACT ON MANAGERS

As more managers have workstations on their own desks, they may be coming to appreciate their potential vulnerability.

It is important to ascertain the true management risk associated with computer viruses, to provide a comprehensible explanation of the problem, and to suggest management approaches to minimising threats. The resulting analysis is likely to draw on both medical analogies and strategic grids.

Computer viruses are more than a problem of technology, but have a critical social dimension. This is not to say, as was originally argued, that computer viruses are transmitted on the sandals of the programmer. As computers and information technology become omnipresent, the behaviour of every employee is relevant, and the same holds for most of the company's stakeholders: competitors, customers, Government, the general public, the media and even suppliers.

The response to viruses, security, is also more than a matter of technology. Security is an attitude, a state of mind, and thus management is the key to its achievement.

As we might expect, for every threat to business there is a commercial solution on offer. We see the appearance of a new industry of virus consultants and virus software. Such solutions carry with them further threats, for any technology used by virus-detection programs can be used against them by hackers wanting to detect and disable virus-detection programs. Successful hackers are often hired by the owners of systems they have penetrated, and are poachers-turned-game-keepers.

At present many companies and organisations take an *ad hoc* approach to problems of security, partly because of the cost involved. There is pressure for more concerted action, which would involve redesign and reconfiguration of systems, changes in the law, and the introduction of more secure systems, which, by definition, would not be compatible with present systems.

Management Dilemmas 5

Problems

FACT, FICTION AND VIRTUAL REALITY

The dividing line between fact and fiction has been blurred by the arrival of virtual reality, which for many may become a standard substitute for real experience. In these days of cost control, a simulation is likely to be more financially acceptable than physical activity. The tacit knowledge that derives from experience will erode further.

Can virtual reality prevent IT disasters or make them more likely? Running complex sets of events through a simulation may reduce the level of mistakes on the part of the agent, but depends for its ultimate viability on the accuracy and effectiveness of the model. Where the model involves smoothing of ragged edges and the reconciliation of inconsistencies, it can prove a dangerous illusion.

The term "virtual reality" is dangerous in itself: for the untutored it sounds as if it is virtually, or almost, real. For the expert it is simply an artificial construct. Popular science fades into pseudo-science in the popular press, and promotional articles are designed to sell products of the arcade-game culture under a new label.

ACCOUNTANCY

Accountancy as virtual reality is dangerous for similar reasons: unthinking people can come to believe that balance sheets and financial performance measures have an objective reality, rather than being constructs from an arbitrary, though conventional, model. The conventions are little challenged until the boom falters, the bubble bursts, and the figures turn out to have been illusory.

LAW

The law takes matters a step forward, for it is a codification of convention made into a professional field by the addition of layers of procedural activity. Fact and fiction drop out of consideration; in adversarial contests it is your virtual reality against mine.

PROFESSIONS

Professionals may be seen as custodians of virtual reality systems, of which their professional bodies are the arbiters. In the case of computer science, as Hoare [1980] argued in his Turing Award Lecture, cited earlier, underneath the layers of procedures and features there may be nothing at all; the Emperor may have abdicated, leaving his empty clothes behind.

This argument is not intended to dismiss the utility of virtual reality systems, or of the professions, but to suggest a reconsideration of the status of both. An intelligent reflecting professional may gain insights into her own practice by developing a model, a virtual reality, which opens it to scrutiny, and clarifies the fact that the professional is part of the problems under consideration, as well as part of the solution. We can stand back and look at artificial models, but not respectably use this as a means of escaping critical analysis for our personal conduct.

Senior managers should be able to "walk through" a virtual reality model of their organisation, following information flows and auditing trails, noting the significance of interfaces and standards. For that to be feasible, there needs to be a foundation of knowledge and a shared vocabulary that encompasses management and technical matters.

Professionals

If you dissemble sometimes your knowledge of that you are thought to know, you shall be thought, another time, to know that you know not.

Francis Bacon (1561–1626)

In the complex world where business and information technology come together, it is not possible for any one person to know everything that needs to be known.

KNOWING WHAT YOU DON'T KNOW

IT disasters will often arise from key people not knowing particular important things, and not being aware that they don't know. As areas of responsibility change in a period of business turbulence, managers may have critical gaps in knowledge of areas for which they are responsible.

It is much easier in hindsight for consultants to identify the causes of a disaster than it is at the time for participants to see what is going wrong. It does not follow that the consultant, given the problem to manage, would perform any better than those in post. A key ability is to know when one does not know what one is doing; to know who to ask for advice; to know when to ask; to know how the request should be phrased; and to know what to do with the answer.

At the heart of areas of difficulty there are often problems of language. The same words may be used with different meanings by people in the business and IT cultures, but without the kind of dialogue that would expose these differences. Lack of overlap of the cultures, by background and by career experience, may mean that limited dialogue has taken place, which would enable understanding to develop regarding meanings and commitments. In cases of doubt, there may be a tacit agreement to close ranks against external interests, resulting in resistance to links.

It is easier for professionals to keep to a culturally homogeneous context, until things go wrong that require interaction with and intervention by others with a distinct and poorly understood culture. There can be particular problems, where trust has not been developed across the cultures, when it appears that others do not know what they are doing.

TRUST

The fundamental concept in the prevention of IT disasters appears to be trust. This can be hard to develop, for one needs to learn by experience where investments of trust are repaid. The earlier one commences such experience the better, as it is best if one's disappointments are not terminal, or even disastrous. Competitive advantage is facilitated by appropriate collaboration, which must be learned.

A disaster may be defined as a failure of trust in a situation that has grave consequences. The trust may have been in a system, a technology, a theology, a Government or an individual. Any recipient of trust will have its limits, though they may not be known or understood. It is clearly advisable therefore to have a feeling for the strengths and limitations of a system, person, or institution before placing great trust in it without recourse to alternatives.

RELATIONSHIPS

On this argument a disaster is a failure of relationships, possibly linked to deficiencies in knowledge. These deficiencies may result from a number of causes:

- Security and confidentiality restrictions may impede the flow of information needed to support mature decisions.
- Individuals may lack the conceptual framework and experience to make use of information available to them.
- Status differences may impede mature discussions between individuals needing to share knowledge.
- The potential disaster situation may be part of a wider problem or network of circumstances, with unknown linkages, side-effects and associated consequences.
- Certain principles may be taken as above or beyond criticism, as tenets of faith, of fundamental ideological beliefs.

EDUCATION

A key insight of computer education concerns the lessons that can be learnt from failure and from awareness of the limits of one's knowledge, language and tools. Debugging is seen as an important intellectual exercise, and it is noted that to aspire to writing bug-free programs is unrealistic.

One outcome of this educational tradition has been a degree of self-awareness, of humility learned through experience of the lessons of failure in a supported environment.

It could be argued that this educational experience is of considerable value, and fundamental to development as a mature professional in our modern technological culture. Significantly, this approach contrasts with that of the modern management culture, where the "can do" culture has encouraged the myth that there are no problems, only opportunities, and that business systems can be put into place to provide reliable solutions that have previously required the exercise of judgement by mature professionals.

Beneath this contrast lies a clash of cultures and expectations, exacerbated all too often by short-term financial pressures. Preventing IT disasters depends on recognising and learning to live with such clashes and pressures. It would be as much a mistake to believe that all such issues could be resolved as it is to believe that IT systems could work infallibly in the real world.

The best way, therefore, to prevent disasters is to avoid placing excessive reliance on individuals or systems, and to develop a mature understanding of strengths, weaknesses and alternatives. For some people this will involve major changes in their approaches to knowledge, systems and organisations.

ATLANTIC COMPUTERS

British and Commonwealth was the star financial services conglomerate of the 1980s, but suddenly collapsed in 1990. It was brought down by the crash of its subsidiary, Atlantic Computers.

Inspectors appointed in June 1990 by the Department of Trade and Industry reported in July 1994, with messages for other big companies who may be tempted to buy firms whose business they do not understand.

British and Commonwealth paid £408 million for a company that was not only worthless, but laden with horrendous liabilities, the inspectors found. Atlantic Computers had never, in its 15-year history, made significant profits in any meaningful sense. The inspectors' report accuses the company of inflating paper earnings by "imprudent" accounting, and says the business and the product being sold were fundamentally unsound. Eventually, Atlantic crashed into insolvency in April 1990, and, one month later, dragged the whole B&C group down with it. The collapse marked the start of the 1990s depression, and sent shock waves through business and industry.

The inspectors note that B&C's advisers, including merchant bankers Barclays de Zoete Wedd, failed to alert B&C to the parlous condition of Atlantic and that B&C, after paying £408 million for the company, adopted a "hands off" approach that allowed the problems to mount. When Atlantic's huge liabilities came to light, the B&C chief executive, John Gunn, and two colleagues kept the knowledge from the Board and from the auditors. They allowed "grossly misleading" profit figures to remain on record, and eventually had to write off practically their entire investment in Atlantic, by that time £485 million, half B&C's total net assets.

So what was the problem with Atlantic Computers?

In 1975 Atlantic was formed to lease computers to industry. Their central product was a highly attractive leasing package called Flexlease. Under its terms, a firm could lease a computer for, typically, six years, and enjoy two important rights: after three years it could demand a new computer, and after five years it could walk away from the lease.

The inspectors noted that Flexlease "gave rise to large potential liabilities for Atlantic". These liabilities were effectively covered by anticipating profits on future leases, "an unsound basis for a long-term business". The inspectors believe that Flexlease was not a viable product, and could not have been transformed into one.

Atlantic's accounting policies helped to disguise the situation. In particular, no advance provision was made against customers exercising their options either to demand new equipment or to "walk". Had conventional accounting been used, the inspectors noted, no significant profits would have been reported at any stage of Atlantic's life.

In 1983, Atlantic floated on the London Stock Exchange. The reporting accountants, Spicer & Pegler, decided that the lack of provisions against liability was acceptable. The inspectors noted that Spicers accepted on the basis of "wholly inadequate" investigations that "walk" options existed in only 5% of Atlantic leases. The true figure was between 60% and 90%. Had Spicers unearthed this, said the inspectors, "it is unlikely that the flotation would have proceeded".

B&C, which was looking for an acquisition, approached Atlantic in mid-1988. Its purchase of Atlantic was made "without a clear understanding of Flexlease". B&C's approach was "marked by inadequate inquiry into Atlantic". At the same time, Atlantic's statements to B&C regarding its liabilities "were incorrect and misleading".

The B&C collapse has triggered numerous legal actions. The company's administrators have extracted a £100 million court award plus £71 million interest from the merchant bank Samuel Montagu, which had been involved in a separate deal in which B&C bought a financial group. B&C's administrators are thought to be planning a £1 billion writ against Atlantic Computers itself, and they have issued a writ against BZW for a sum thought to exceed £500 million for its role in the Atlantic affair.

Some simple conclusions can be drawn from this damaging affair:

- The purchase of Atlantic Computers was driven by financial engineering, the quest for earnings to support B&C shares.
- The leasing system was fundamentally flawed, allowing buyers to trade-in their computers at any time on the basis that traded-in computers had some resale value.
- Neither the merchant bank, BZW, nor the auditors, Spicer & Pegler, now part of Touche Ross, understood the flaky nature of the business. Everybody blames everybody else, insisting it was someone else's responsibility to investigate the underlying business.
- The rapid pace of change in the technological and business environment of the IT industry makes it a dangerous arena for operations by those who do not understand either the technology or business issues.
- In Britain's stock-market-based system, everyone's concern is with finance, and nobody's with the business. The big profits are made by trading assets, auditing them and financing them. Atlantic Computers is a spectacular example of how the system goes wrong; but the more dangerous problem is that the contagion of financial engineering affects our entire business establishment.

Panaceas

I hold that the characteristic of the present age is craving credulity.

Benjamin Disraeli (1804–81), 25th November 1864

Technical breakthroughs, and the sudden affordability of powerful computer systems, led to some unfulfilled hopes for solutions to business problems, as research met the real world. It was hoped by some that mathematical logic would provide the foundations for a new generation of computer systems, solving problems of knowledge and of computer interfaces.

LOGIC AND DECLARATIVE SYSTEMS

The Japanese Fifth Generation Computer Systems project of the 1980s took logic programming as its unifying concept, and PROLOG as the starting point for a core language. This external vote of confidence encouraged British and European researchers to make a radical reappraisal of programming methodology and software technology, announcing what amounted to the dawn of a new age, where hardware constraints would no longer be dominant.

Logic programming, and related technologies of automatic programming, offered potential solutions to "the software crisis", which was crippling business operations.

The outcomes of the project were not fully fledged commercial systems, but advances in the development of a new generation of hardware and software. Those who hoped for the early availability of low-cost artificial intelligence business applications systems have been disappointed. The scaling down or abandonment of major research and development programmes, such as the Alvey Programme in the UK, reduces the chances of such developments.

NEURAL NETWORKS

Frustrated by the limitations of conventional computing systems, an increasing number of companies are turning to neural networks. Supposedly based on the same design principles as the human brain, neural networks have shown themselves capable of "learning", improving their performance in solving problems through a series of examples.

Applications include monitoring station platforms to see if they are too crowded, looking at the behaviour of international financial markets and currency movements, predicting company failures, and providing translations.

THE DANGERS OF THE BLACK BOX

The potential benefits are great, but only a few have appreciated the dangers, and they may be restricted to a proportion of technical users. Neural networks are used in areas where conventional systems and rule-based approaches have failed, and cannot give explanations of their conclusions. They remain black boxes, and users will continue with them if they find their conclusions satisfactory.

What has been insufficiently understood is that neural networks need to be considered in the context of expert knowledge. When asking a question to a neural network, it is vital to know what would count as a sensible answer, and what considerations could affect the outcome, what knowledge was available, and what information was beyond the reach of the system.

To rely on a black box is to abdicate management control.

We have seen the dangers of inappropriate automation in the use of programmed trading systems in Wall Street, designed to trigger decisions to buy or sell when particular indices or patterns are discerned. Programmed trading can precipitate a major crash, as systems feed on themselves, setting up a vicious spiral.

We may classify such machine-encouraged traumas as IT disasters, but the roots of such situations lie in human conduct and frailty. It may be easier for the self-respect of managers for them to welcome the inputs from an advanced technology system than to enter into critical discussions that reveal their ignorance.

Neural networks have great potential as a management tool, suggesting new areas for research and activity, but they depend on a strong foundation of knowledge on the part of users. Without the investment in knowledge, the technology could prove disastrous.

INTELLIGENT AGENTS

International consultancies are now looking beyond the artificial intelligence systems of the 1980s, and the new hardware and software architectures that were stimulated by major research and development programmes such as the Japanese Fifth Generation programme. Object-oriented software has reached commercial applications, and beyond it lies the development of "intelligent agents, objects that think". Ovum see the new technology as set to revolutionise both telecommunications and IT, in both systems and services. Intelligent agents are seen as task-oriented software components that have the ability to act intelligently, either independently or collectively.

Early users of intelligent agents are already demonstrating dramatic improvements in several important application areas, including:

- Electronic mail
- Network management

- Workflow systems
- User interfaces
- Information retrieval
- Modelling/simulation

Because the technologies and applications for intelligent agents are so new, the answers to many questions remain uncertain. What are the technological options, and how should potential users choose between them? Yet again, disastrous fates await those who choose unwisely!

Method

In theory, many problems have been solved by technical means, and the application of methods.

Systems development methodologies are intended to work independently of software packages, but themselves impose a programmed mode of working that can conflict with the demands of complex problems, and of complex organisations.

There is a well established school of thought that the solution to the software crisis, and to problems of "software pollution", is system development according to prescribed methods. Following on from structured programming, advocates of methods try to separate systems analysis from the activity of coding, and to develop common approaches across teams.

RISK ANALYSIS

They now add a methodical approach to risk. An IT security risk analysis programme is regarded as essential for adequate IT protection. The first step is to identify and assess the value to the organisation of the assets, particularly data and information, which comprise the system under review. This should be expressed in business terms, e.g. what would be the effects on the business were services to be suddenly made unavailable, if the system was destroyed or sensitive data disclosed or modified in an unauthorised way.

The next step is to identify the threats, both deliberate and accidental, that might manifest against the assets, and to assess their likelihood. Then the vulnerabilities or weaknesses of the system must be identified, and their degree of seriousness assessed.

The combination of all these factors, i.e. business impact or asset valuation, threat and vulnerability assessment, enables the risks to be measured. This is the essence of risk analysis. The subsequent stage of risk management identifies countermeasures appropriate to the assessed risks.

The Government technical advisory body CCTA make brave claims for the CRAMM system [CCTA 1990], intended to strengthen security measures:

"It is a complete method for identifying and justifying all the necessary protective measures to ensure the security of both current and future information technology systems used for processing valuable or sensitive data."

Without the use of such systems, they argue:

"Businesses are increasingly at risk through use of the very tool bought to increase efficiency, i.e. IT." *(p. 7)*

Automation

The history of industrialisation has been about the automation of a succession of processes. Computing, which brought automation to many manual and clerical functions, is itself open to automation. We may come to see the first generations of programmers as the hand loom weavers of the second industrial revolution.

With the development of the mathematics of programming, and of programming languages with a mathematical foundation, it becomes more possible to talk of automatic programming, whereby a program is generated from a specification.

CASE

CASE tools are intended to automate the demanding process of software development, using software assistance, and building-in the requirements of particular standards.

Martin and Maclure [1990] have argued that CASE is software automation, and have hailed the prospect of reliable, reusable software, while at the same time freeing managers from the necessity of programming or understanding programming.

Reverse engineering is intended to enable the software engineer to dismantle and rationally reconstruct packages derived from other sources. Such techniques, however, do not permit the reconstruction of the organisational and business cultural context in which the original package was developed. There is a further complication. If the reverse engineering is too effective, clinical or obvious, it can be regarded as copyright infringement, and made the subject of major legal actions.

Bibel [1989] argued against regarding CASE as providing the answer to problems of complexity:

"CASE is built on the concept of reusing parts of previously built functional systems, modules as they are called in the jargon, within newly developed systems. While this idea is not wrong wherever it would happen that such a module more or less by chance would indeed fit as a part in the new system, it certainly does not provide a remedy for the main problem of the complexity and inflexibility of executive systems."

Developing software is a risky business. Major organisations have encountered problems of critical applications delivered late or over budget, or, worst of all, crashing due to undetected software errors.

SOFTWARE TESTING

There is no way around the necessity for rigorous testing of software. The consultants Ovum state:

"No matter how sophisticated the development methods or tools, systematic and extensive testing at all stages of the development life-cycle remains the only way to ensure high standards of quality in software development. Such testing needs to address issues of functionality, performance and user acceptability."

Help is, however, at hand, as parts of the software testing process can themselves be automated:

"Until recently, software testing has been a purely manual process, making it time-consuming, monotonous, unreliable and, not surprisingly, unpopular with development staff."

As we might expect, there are vendors eager to sell us products:

"Now there is a wide range of CAST (Computer-Aided Software Testing) tools, aiming to automate some or all of the testing process. CAST tools can cut the time spent testing by 30% or more whilst achieving far higher levels of accuracy. But choosing the right tool, or combination of tools, is a daunting challenge. Moreover, many corporate IT developers do not have experience in evaluating CAST tools, meaning that valuable time and resources may be spent in inappropriate testing."

As before, it is a question of offering power tools to those who lack the intellectual maturity to use them responsibly.

Those concerned with the developing profession of software engineering, such as Bott *et al.* [1991], have concern that the use of analogical language, making software development seem straightforward, could cause confusion among the unwary and non-specialist population:

"As a result of efforts to make the development of software less uncertain and more disciplined, it has become fashionable to use analogies such as the 'software factory' and to talk about software development in terms of production management. While this trend is desirable, it is easy to be misled by the analogies. Production management is concerned with the replication of a product; software development is concerned with the development of new products. In particular, the

lack of effective and usable 'software metrics', despite the considerable research activity in this area, makes it very difficult to use quantitative techniques." (p. 19)

The expensive seminars by confident consultants continue, and presenters maintain that your software would be safe with them: why not choose them for your outsourcing contract?

People

SOFTWARE ENGINEERS

The danger derives not just from the software systems, but from the incompetence with which they are developed and used. This is the depressing conclusion of the report on *Undergraduate Curricula for Software Engineering* [BCS/IEE 1989]:

"Although software products do not degrade, human intervention may degrade them. They depend on the environment and cannot without renewed tests of fitness for purpose be transferred to environments other than those for which they were designed." (p. 12)

Method is lacking not only in software development, but in software engineering as a profession:

"The software produced by people whose principal skill is in another discipline is often a prototype, suitable for demonstrating feasibility, but unsuited to production and sustained use." (p. 13)

The field has developed at great speed, without laying firm foundations:

"Some of the intellectual tools and methods of software engineering are at present skills in process of development, and rapid change is to be expected for some time to come. Software engineers therefore need the theoretical understanding which will be a foundation for learning and using new methods in the future, and the cast of mind which sees the constant updating of knowledge as required professional behaviour." (p. 14)

Formal methods are intended to provide a rigorous mathematical foundation for software developed for business use. The problem is that formal methods presupposed a degree of mathematical sophistication that is rare in business. Consequently, officially imposed standards have had to be withdrawn as they could not be met.

ERROR-FREE SOFTWARE

With the prevalence of professional weakness, software cannot reach its full potential. Baber [1991] argues for the possibility of error-free software:

"Errors in software are avoidable design errors: human errors on the part of the software developer. They are not inherent in the nature of software." (p. 8)

It would be mistaken to look for error-free software in light of current practices:

"Developing in the traditional way software upon which human life depends is nothing other than high tech Russian roulette." (p. 123)

SOFTWARE REUSE

Walton and Maiden [1993] have shown that the cause of software reuse, as a means of increasing reliability, has been frustrated by poor management:

"Many previous attempts to introduce software reuse into organisations have failed due to their focus on single reuse issues, such as retrieval or generification of modules or due to their mishandling of sensitive management and human issues, such as the Not Invented Here (NIH) syndrome." (p. viii)

Walton and Dettwiler [1993, p. 1] point out that the reasons for failure are normally not predominantly technical, but "psychological, sociological, or economic". Also, they write that:

"The needs of the organisation are best served by pooling valuable pieces of knowledge (in the form of reusable components) and making that knowledge widely available." (p. 3)

Reekie [1993] points out that software reuse can only succeed as part of an overall planned production process:

"Component management can only work where, instead of manufacturing software in response to the arising of demand, we manufacture parts in anticipation of future demand. The burden of software's diversity moves from manufacture to assembly, which is why it needs technology such as object orientation with a low impact of change and a high level of reuse." (p. 49)

Sutcliffe [1993] advises caution in the face of bold promises from advocates of formal methods:

"The outlook for reuse is not promising. Optimistically, the considerable effort put into object oriented methods and tools may start to bear fruit, but this does not address the vast mass of existing software, unless a reverse engineering exercise is undertaken on the software maintenance mountain. Formal methods cannot provide a silver bullet for object orientation or specification of modular software." (p. 69)

PROJECT MANAGEMENT

Brooks has memorably established that project management, and the successful delivery of working software systems, is not simply a matter of individual mastery of technology [Brooks 1975]:

"Other people set one's objectives, provide one's resources, and furnish one's information. One rarely controls the circumstances of his work, or even its goal. In management terms, one's authority is not sufficient for his responsibility. In practice, actual (as opposed to formal) authority is acquired from the very momentum of accomplishment." (p. 8)

The challenges are real and practical, rather than theoretical:

"The obsolescence of an implementation must be measured against other existing implementations, not against unrealised concepts. The challenge and the mission are to find real solutions to real problems on actual schedules with available resources." (p. 9)

When problems arise, just adding more effort may not be the answer:

"When a task cannot be partitioned because of sequential constraints, the application of more effort has no effect on the schedule." (p. 17)

With complex problems involving a number of participants, particularly when they are working at scattered sites, the overhead burden of communication should not be underestimated:

"In tasks that can be partitioned but which require communication among the subtasks, the effort of communication must be added to the amount of work to be done." (p. 17)

Frank Land has summed up the problem of overemphasising the technical dimension, when considering the process of technology transfer from designer to user [Land 1992]:

"None of the standard methodologies pays serious attention to the problem of technology transfer from design and construction to user." (p. 113)

Standards

BRINGING COMPONENTS TOGETHER

Developing complex systems requires the agreement of standards, enabling different components of the overall system to fit together. Fortunes are to be made from establishing standards in, for example, operating systems or microprocessor design, providing a target for implementers to address with applications.

What is the place of standards? What should we standardise, and how? Having agreed standards, how can they be enforced, and with what sanctions? More difficult, how can the transition between standards be managed? How can different standards coexist, either as an interim or longer-term arrangement?

Given that each standard evolves over time to meet a given set of circumstances and requirements, there can be difficulties in bringing together systems with different standards. The founder users of Unix would not have happily coexisted with IBM computer centre managers, and this is not a matter to be resolved by technical means alone.

Unix assumed a degree of familiarity with computer systems and languages, and a relative indifference to interface design issues. By contrast, the designers of the Macintosh assumed a more graphical style of use, rather than conventional programming at the command level.

The IBM PC epitomised the standard new-generation office equipment, supporting business users. Office procedures could be followed on a series of packages and integrated suites. The *de facto* standard for a number of years was therefore the current version of the Intel microprocessor, the current version of Microsoft DOS, and the dominant word-processing, database and spreadsheet packages. In each case the standard defined the interface, not the precise tools to be used by the individual. Clones of the IBM PC have outsold the IBM product, and competing software packages offered import and export capabilities.

UPGRADING

The challenge of upgrades and compatibility has faced both users and vendors, with varying degrees of success. Each new product has been under pressure to offer compatibility with predecessors, and to provide a basis for future development. Vendors have part of their product specification predetermined: the problem is to meet it, while coping with the constraints of the memory capacity of the entry-level and dominant models in the target range, and offering new features that exceed the performance of competitor products. After many years of incremental upgrading within the IBM PC culture, the question is whether companies and organisations can cope with a wholesale change. A change to Unix graphics workstations, for example, would require discontinuity at the applications level as well as hardware level. Workstation vendors such as Sun Microsystems have not seen it as a priority to offer business applications such as WordPerfect, demonstrating a lack of understanding of the business culture and its needs.

THE PERILS OF CHANGE

Counting the Cost

In these cost-conscious days, there is pressure within all organisations to watch the bottom line. Every expenditure must be justified in terms of return on investment, and when presented with a package of items, there is a tendency to choose only the most essential. An alternative is to break down the overall budget into small enough items to avoid the most demanding processes of justification.

Thus, by hook or by crook, companies and other organisations have achieved first-generation computerisation by the piecemeal purchase of personal computers. Only the most scrupulous have ensured that all software in use is fully covered by licences. The perceived high cost of maintenance contracts and the rapid rate of obsolescence of generations of processors have been cited in support of strategies of repair on demand and replacement. Management have avoided recruiting expensive specialist staff or retraining the current workforce, noting the claims of vendors that even grandmothers can use the full range of business software.

Organisations have survived for a number of years on this basis, as technology has become more widespread, and upgrading has been possible between generations of processors and versions of software packages. Specialist technical groups have been broken up and dispersed, as the need for centralised computing has been perceived as declining, offering welcome savings. Technical considerations have been dismissed as priority has been given to the needs of business.

Technological change is not always gradual and continuous, with guaranteed compatibility and portability. Computing, and the use of computers in organisations, has been such a recent development that few have experience of managing major change.

We can identify particular patterns of problems that, if not handled sensibly, can lead to disaster.

Windows

After a decade of systems using successive versions of DOS for personal computers, new users have come to expect access to MS Windows on a PC with at least a 486 microprocessor, together with a suite of memory-hungry business packages. Indeed, such systems are sold as entry-level systems to primary schools and home computer users.

For organisations that have sought to provide computers for all their key staff over a period of years, and where there is a requirement for a consistent environment across the organisation, there are uncomfortable choices. Either the users of newly acquired systems have to accept less than the current industry standards in order to remain compatible with earlier systems; or industry standards are observed by that proportion of the organisation who are properly equipped; or, finally, the organisation faces a major bill for wholesale replacement of systems that are declared to be obsolete.

At Kingston Business School we have sought to steer something of a middle way, managing the IT resource as a whole, and allocating newly acquired equipment to those with specialist requirements. Equipment has been recycled through the organisation, catering for the needs of heavy number-crunchers as well as those who are only concerned with word processing. All staff and students have access to compatible systems, networked locally and with the University and wider world.

Given that the rest of the University were later in adopting personal computers, and have given less priority for open access on a large scale, it has been reasonable for the central computing service to recommend current standards for operating systems and packages. As Government has been late in determining budgets for capital equipment, and has provided sums corresponding to some 20% of the cost of implementing agreed strategies, the Business School will be unable to comply with University standards.

The forced maintaining of several different standards places a considerable additional burden on the technical support function. Expertise is required to ensure the transfer of critical data and files between applications. It is not enough to have a few specialist support staff; users need to understand the constraints of the environment in which they are working.

Workstations

Technical change and the declining cost of hardware have reduced the price differential between the most expensive personal computer and the bottom of the range of graphics workstations, previously restricted to specialist scientific and technical users. There has been the temptation to dip the toe in the water, and gain experience of the culture of workstation use. There has been a lack of appreciation of the nature of that "culture", and how it differs from the culture of personal computers in a business environment.

Vendors of workstations are accustomed to selling to users with an interest in the technology, and with the expertise to cope with the challenges of installation and system management. Military and scientific laboratories will be used to negotiating maintenance contracts, and to the vagaries of software systems under development. Individual users may enjoy customising their own interfaces and local environments, relishing the facilities provided by an advanced operating system.

By contrast, modern businesses like systems to work first time, in their own local environment, meeting the needs of business without requiring users to be expert in the technology and fluent in technical jargon. They expect to find their usual business software packages "bundled in" with the hardware on delivery, and do not expect to have to finance either maintenance contracts or specialist technical support.

Market leaders in the workstation market saw the opportunity to bridge the culture gap by offering a software environment that could support both Unix and Windows software. However, with early releases, this both ran business packages much slower than on personal computers, and required high-specification workstations in order to run. The difference between the technical and business perspectives remains.

There is no such thing as a free lunch, or a free network of Unix workstations. Even if the initial hardware is provided free of charge, the costs of maintenance contracts and of both hardware and software upgrades rapidly mount up, quickly consuming declining capital equipment budgets.

Client–Server

After the eras of mainframe computers, clusters of minicomputers, and the turbulent years of personal computers, there is general agreement that the dominant architecture for the next decade is client–server, with users having access to powerful database systems in an open environment. On the positive side, such an arrangement combines distributed processing with many of the best features of managed computer centres. However, if a client–server approach is adopted in a networked environment of disparate user workstations, there are considerable dangers when changes are made without taking full account of their effects across the system.

There comes a time when it seems prudent to upgrade the operating system on a major server, with practical implications for all users. Full compatibility cannot be guaranteed, and changes in protocols to meet one set of needs may prejudice the effective working of others. Peripheral devices such as printers may have to be modified for the new operating system, rendering them unable to continue their previous functions under the old system.

It is normally possible to test the efficacy of individual upgrading changes within an experimental setting, but prediction of the impact of changes on a system-wide basis would require expensive and exhaustive testing, based on a level of detailed knowledge of individual user requirements that has largely disappeared in the era of distributed processing and end-user computing. Management, and not just IT management, has to address the problems that result from the loss of access to critical applications, or pressure to change modes of working in order to adjust to the demands of changing technology. A casual, reactive approach to IT management is no longer sufficient, but a directive approach may provoke opposition and cultural discontinuity.

MANAGING AMID TECHNICAL CHANGE

It becomes apparent from these three patterns of problems, which can arise at the same time, that the critical area for investment is in the human resource. Management cannot devolve the burden of technical understanding to a small specialist group, but must accept the responsibility of remaining abreast of technological change so that they have insights into the technical dimension of business decisions. It is no answer to announce that business considerations will drive technical decisions if the technical implications are not understood by decision-makers.

Universities exist to develop the human resource, yet senior management who determine the strategic direction of the organisation may lack technical expertise, and there may be no representation of such concerns at executive level. The consequence can be corporate incoherence, inadequacies in information management and expensive mistakes. To rectify such problems requires root-and-branch reconsideration of fundamental processes, and a preparedness to reorganise institutional structures in order to secure improvements.

EXISTING APPLICATIONS

One of the challenges facing developers of expert systems, knowledge-based systems and improved database management systems has been to address concerns over the vast past investment in IT applications, often written in COBOL, for which wholesale rewriting was impracticable. There will be existing products and practices to take into account, and the corresponding vested interests to contend with and to try to reconcile.

GROUPWARE

An effective standard in place across an organisation can have revolutionary impact, as is being claimed for a number of rival groupware products, providing a common communication environment. Groupware, when successfully implemented, can combine computer technology and an understanding of workgroup pressures.

The use of groupware addressing a common standard can unlock the power of information, the lifeblood of modern organisations. Groupware facilitates the shift in information ethics, from the notion that information is power that needs to be withheld, to the understanding that shared information and learning is empowerment.

The problems of change are not to be underestimated, but the benefits look likely to be considerable. People and their organisations change slowly. The lead time to learn new ways of working will be invaluable to those companies that master new group technologies. Enthusiasts argue that groupware will define the form of post-industrial society. Just as the assembly line has become the metaphor for the industrial age, groupware could well become the metaphor for the post-industrial age.

The critical requirement is clear thinking in the organisation concerned. Experience suggests that the effective use of groupware requires clarity of purpose, alignment with a common goal and commitment to results. Underpinning all of this must be a degree of technical understanding at senior levels of the organisation.

SECURITY

The UK IT and electronics industry has long been dominated by the needs of defence. A strong premium has been placed on security, which is at the heart of the objectives of defence policy overall. With the ending of the Cold War, the diminution of major defence contracts and the increasingly competitive nature of the IT market, defence software companies have had to look for civil applications of their areas of defence expertise.

An obvious focus of attention is security, and security evaluation. The argument, as put by EDS (Electronic Data Systems, founded by Ross Perot and now owned by General Motors), is deceptively simple:

> *"Government departments have well established measures to provide adequate protection to information which affects national interests. These measures address physical and administrative security, and, in the case of information systems, technical security is necessary to safeguard, for example, office, command, control, communications and combat systems.*
>
> *Commercial enterprises also recognise their own security needs to protect sensitive information, avoid unauthorised access and to guard against the damaging consequences of fraud, sabotage or computer viruses.*
>
> *Each organisation has its own particular requirements for protection dependent upon the security and/or integrity associated with its IT systems. Hence, there is a need to establish the degree of trust that can be placed on the implementation of security measures such that the diverse range of requirements are met by corresponding levels of protection. Also, there is a need for a standardised and independent means by which confidence in IT security features can be determined. These principles apply equally to both off the shelf systems and bespoke systems. As a result, security evaluation criteria have been developed to provide a coherent approach to development and assessment of product or system trustworthiness."*

They have, therefore, established a CLEF (Commercial Licence Evaluation Facility), with Government blessing:

> *"All systems and products to be evaluated require a statement on their security aspects, a security target, which expresses the level of assurance required and the functional computer security requirements. The role of the CLEF is to test the security target to ensure that the necessary trusted functions are correctly implemented and complete."*

The Government has instituted a scheme of certification:

> *"Scheme certification can be used by vendors to advertise and sell their products. Systems integrators have a measure of confidence in the security features offered by component products, and may not need to evaluate all parts of their complete system; thus reducing risks, costs, and timescales. End-users can be confident that their systems meet security targets and provide the necessary protection of sensitive information, whilst maintaining authorised access. In the future, it is expected that European policy decisions will set the minimum level of protection*

for IT systems in government and commercial sectors in terms of the evaluation criteria."

EDS–Scicon provides a wide range of services in support of this approach:

- Advice on the scheme, and the evaluation process.
- Consultancy support to define security requirements and develop a security policy.
- Conduct of initial audits to identify any readily apparent shortcomings.
- Support to procurement processes and procedures.
- Production of security specifications and assessments of supplier contributions.
- Independent advice on security issues to developers and suppliers; threat and risk analysis, and security policies; advice on how to meet end-users' requirements.
- Consultancy on the use of special techniques associated with the development and evaluation of secure systems and products; advice on the use of formal methods and tool-based verification and validation.

One major outcome of this approach has been the award to EDS of the contract to run the IT operations of the Inland Revenue, although they face complex software licensing disputes with, for example, Computer Associates. They have favoured status with DTI and the Government communications centre, GCHQ, and must expect further business.

Quality

Software quality may be critical for systems effectiveness, and even for the survival of human users, yet it is hard to define and quantify. Though it is easy to demand quality and complete reliability, management alone is not enough. It is no more possible to manage quality into a software product than it is to test it in.

TAYLOR ON SCIENTIFIC MANAGEMENT

Taylor's approach to management was based on the division of labour and top-down control. Workers operated in a stable environment with clear job descriptions. The principles of management could be expressed as scientific principles [Taylor 1911]:

1. Develop a science for each element of a man's work to replace the old rule-of-thumb method.

2. Scientifically select and then train, teach and develop the workman.
3. Cooperate with the men so as to ensure that all the work would be done in accordance with scientific principles.
4. Divide responsibility between management and workmen. Management takes over all functions for which they are better fitted than the workmen.

This approach is less appropriate to the knowledge-based activity of software development and maintenance, in flatter, less hierarchical organisations, where responsibilities and communications are less clearly vertically defined.

COMPANY CULTURE

In conventional management there is the commitment both to learning on the job through practical experience, and to "getting it right first time, every time". Enlightened consultants will look for evidence that a company tolerates errors, and encourages its staff to explore new ideas and approaches, as a key part of company culture.

The early "quality gurus" placed emphasis on company culture, and looked to approaches such as quality circles to raise collective awareness. Deming [1982] pointed to the high costs of poor management, which failed to plan, and wasted manpower, materials and machine time, resulting in increased prices and loss of market share.

Deming would not recognise his principles in the current obsession with documentation as a substitute for practice; he would note consistency and conformity as the new virtues, coupled with a return to the Taylorist approach to scientific management, concern with which had prompted the quality movement in the first place.

SOFTWARE ENGINEERING MANAGEMENT

Tom Gilb saw software engineering management in terms of quality issues. He dismissed excuses for accidents, seeing them as entirely attributable to management. He saw the need to use powerful tools for thinking, moving on from traditional approaches, and recognising the nature of the underlying problem of communication between people.

He addresses the problem of incompetence, and how to minimise the damage [Gilb 1988]:

> "If you intend to fail, or fear that failure is inevitable, then stick to unclear goals to hide your incompetence." (p. 30)

Disarmingly, he suggests that management confidence is often a facade:

"Experts know they don't know, the others try to fool people that they do."
(p. 194)

Profits and Prophets

PAYMENT BY RESULTS

In whatever section of the economy, the trend has been to move to a focus on outcomes, to payment by results. Funding agencies do not wish to be bothered by details of modes of delivery of the product or service and they wish to drive down the costs of inputs by applying rigid cash limits to the payment for outputs. Control is thus with the funding agency while responsibility remains with the contracted organisation.

One consequence of this shift has been a distortion of the processes of collection and recording of data and information for both internal and external auditing purposes. The funding agency will state, on a basis that may change annually or even more frequently, the performance indicators on which it will rely when deciding financial allocations. This poses pressure on the organisation to reconfigure its published accounts to conform with the current criteria and to maximise income. The same procedures are capable of a number of modes of description depending on external requirements.

What may be lost is a clear understanding, within the organisation itself, of the nature of its working. The rush to meet external demands may be at the expense of local reflection and prioritisation. One answer is to maintain separate records for internal use, but this raises problems in itself. Few staff will have the background and ability to grasp and reconcile different and apparently conflicting accounts. External auditors may demand the right of access to internal accounts, or may, by virtue of IT, have automatic access to such information.

The absurdity of the obsession for specified information is demonstrated in the publication of league tables. Different organisations cited have given different interpretations to the standard questions, and the resulting tabulations are accorded no respect.

The availability of IT strengthens the capacity of Government to demand and present such information, and facilitates the diversion of attention away from inconvenient issues, such as underlying levels of resource provision, requirements for repair and maintenance, and social need.

Learning From Experience

6

If you can keep your head when all about you
Are losing theirs and blaming it on you,
If you can trust yourself when all men doubt you,
But make allowance for their doubting too;
If you can wait and not be tired by waiting,
Or being lied about, don't deal in lies,
Or being hated, don't give way to hating,
And yet don't look too good, not talk too wise;

If you can dream – and not make dreams your master;
If you can think – and not make thoughts your aim;
If you can meet with Triumph and Disaster
And treat those two impostors just the same.

Rudyard Kipling (1865–1936), If

... Then you could take on the role of an IT manager.

Support Services

Individual motorists are advised to join the Automobile Association or the Royal Automobile Club, using their maps, emergency services and specialist advice. In addition, it is prudent to ensure that vehicles receive a regular servicing overhaul from a reputable garage. Drivers of defective vehicles may be breaking the law, and liable for summary and serious punishment. Brake failures through insufficient maintenance, for example, can lead to multiple deaths.

Similar practices and understandings have yet to develop for IT systems. We still find that organisations may have budgeted for the initial hardware and software purchase, but have no funds for ongoing maintenance and licence extensions. Systems continue to be used without proper support, and without recourse to either the IT "garage", or the equivalent of the AA and RAC. As cars come with manuals, and are typically the result of mass production, mechanics are likely to be able to help. On the other hand, IT systems may have been custom-built, often in-house, by well intentioned amateurs. They either lack documentation or the documentation was an *aide memoire* to the system builder, long since departed.

So what is the answer? "User groups" may attract amateur enthusiasts, but in commercial organisations there can be a fear of disclosing critical information to competitors, or of appearing foolish. Professional associations are weak, and the qualifications of IT staff and managers diverse and inconsistent.

In the past it was easy. Nobody got fired for buying IBM. Typically, companies would lease IBM systems, which they would trade-in at regular intervals in order to change to a more powerful system at an increased fee level. The service was all-inclusive, covering hardware, software and applications, with courses available for relevant staff. This was not controversial, as demand, power and chargeable prices rose together in a growing economy.

Today, the answer may be to seek guidance from a systems integrator, who undertakes to bring together the different components, which may be products of many manufacturers, addressing various original standards. However, in these days of commodity hardware and bundled business software packages, it is harder for companies to justify the additional expense of consultancy with no apparent benefit.

At the end of the day, organisations are likely to depend on in-house expertise to determine whether they survive disaster.

SPRINGER-VERLAG, LONDON – CASE STUDY

Springer management decided to install a computer network of about 20 IBM-compatible PCs, so that information could be shared by editors, publishers and production staff. The work was given to a local company (in Wimbledon) that offered a particularly low price for Tulip computers, which they recommended.

The Novell network was installed, with WordPerfect and four laser printers. Printing was erratic, and the network would occasionally crash for no apparent reason. This was irritating, but not disastrous. Various visits by service personnel failed to solve this problem. A tape backup drive was installed. The original supplier went out of business.

Determined to make sure of getting a good service, Springer decided on an expensive maintenance contract (well into four figures) on the system, and placed this with a very large national service organisation (after looking at presentations by several competing companies).

An accounts package was purchased and installed. A database/workflow system was designed, installed and run in parallel with the existing "paper" system for six months. The "paper" system was then discontinued as the database appeared to be working perfectly.

The network continued to behave erratically, despite numerous call-outs to the service company; this was now more serious because Springer was dependent on IT for job-tracking and accounts, as well as for typing. The tape drive started producing data error messages. A service engineer was summoned, and fixed the problem.

The occasional crashes continued, and eventually the service company recommended that the network server be replaced ("Tulips are unreliable as servers"), and the network software be upgraded to the next version. The hard disk (an expensive high-capacity model) was to be reused in the new server. This was agreed.

An engineer arrived with the new server and software, and made two full tape backups of the server hard disk. The disk drive was transferred to the new machine, but when tested appeared to have many bad sectors. A low-level format was performed on it to correct this. Subsequently, the operating system and Netware were successfully mounted.

The whole of Springer's data and software were now (only) on the two backup tapes. Or, rather, they should have been. Remember the engineer who "fixed" the faulty tape drive? He had done it by switching off the error messages that the software was generating, leaving the actual fault uncorrected. Only about 30% of the files on the two tapes were recoverable.

The system was down for three weeks, and business practically ground to a halt. About a week's worth of data were lost from accounts and the database, and *all* the information would have been lost completely had not the Book-keeper and the Editorial Director both kept their own floppy-disk backups.

What could Springer have done to prevent this expensive and damaging disaster?

Postscript: The underlying cause of the erratic behaviour of the network was eventually traced (by another service company) to the original installers having trapped one of the network (Ethernet) cables between a floorboard and a joist, partially severing the wire.

From Computer Centres to Distributed Processing

Kingston University, like many other organisations, has undergone rapid change. Over a short period of time, several generations of information technology have been in use, each with its own culture of use, support and management.

The University was an early pioneer in the use of Digital VAX minicomputers as the basis of a University-wide service based on VMS. The University Computing Service became accustomed to servicing users of VMS, and then Unix.

The advent and proliferation of personal computers meant that Faculties working with industry clients felt under pressure to follow industry developments, even though personal computers based on DOS and then Windows were not integrated into the University environment, and did not then enjoy central technical support.

Although the initial personal computers were stand-alone, pressure has increased for networking, and for integration of the different technologies into an overall University system. Integration needed to include the different varieties of Unix workstation acquired in piecemeal fashion across the University, and had to take account of national and international standards.

As distributed processing became more established, and user expectations rose, there was a need for more formal management and technical support across the organisation. It became possible to distinguish different levels of support needs for which different provision could be made, with necessary links and agreed standards.

Whereas many had seen the development of distributed processing as a means of asserting independence from the central organisation, it became apparent that reliable services required a new degree of discipline and self-discipline, and that this would not come about by chance. The Computing Service was, in effect, reinvented, but with a different role, concerned with maintaining standards and interfaces, and enabling users to manage their own activities without adverse impacts on others. Computing Service Agreements have evolved, subject to regular review by those concerned with the practical delivery of services.

These changes have taken place over a short period of time, and have required a wholesale reappraisal of the roles of individuals and groups within the organisation. Previous organisational structures may be in need of revision. Vertical structures of management and reporting may be replaced by a more horizontal networking approach.

Networking the Organisation

Networks connect more than computers; users, cultures and communities are involved. Networks facilitate links between individuals in a manner that impacts on the working of organisations. Local cultures may be challenged by the intrusion of available alternatives. Management and teaching methods face constant revision, and pressure to share experience and resources, in contrast to the traditional individualist approach. Established staff may feel insecure and threatened.

As procedures adapt to take advantage of technical advances, organisations do not survive unchanged. Where software is shared and messages are distributed by electronic mail, ways of working are altered. If the new facilities collapse or are perceived as unreliable, the organisation can be destabilised. Kingston University has experienced a long legacy of disillusion with the University Management Information System, whose failings prompted individual faculties to evolve their own database systems to meet their pressing local needs. There is now the challenge of reintegrating these distributed components, preserving the breadth of ownership of working systems.

As separate Faculties across the University networked their computers and sought to take advantage of electronic mail, both internal and external, they encountered the need to agree standards, compromising local plans in order to achieve more general advances. Technology could not be the principal driver, for users would not necessarily have access to the latest state-of-the-art hardware and software, given an overall context of budgetary constraints. In the Business School, for example, there are several hundred workstations, which require a consistent software environment and interface. Upgrading of software becomes a management problem to ensure continuity across the organisation. Opportunities arise for better control of problems, and monitoring of usage, protection against piracy and viruses.

User involvement is critical. Those who have been directly involved in network installation projects have learnt that only when there is direct end-user participation in the design and implementation phases will the system be accepted by people, and be able to deliver the productivity benefits that justify the up-front investment. Networking has to be seen as supporting the work of the faculty or organisation concerned. The information network must complement the company culture, not replace it. In other words it must mesh properly with the way things are done in the organisation from a human perspective, so that the particular glue that binds together the individuals and workgroups in the company is reinforced, not weakened.

IT Strategy as a Process

The conventional view of IT strategy is that it is something determined "on high", with competitive advantage in mind, and then promulgated down the layers of the organisation. Strategic deliberations are followed by implementation and evaluation.

In practice, this model is not adequate, for those at the senior executive level of most organisations do not have direct responsibility for IT, having delegated the function to a more junior specialist. Senior executives lack understanding of and familiarity with many of the technical issues, and are preoccupied with the need to reduce costs. Corporate strategies are developed without taking major account of IT, and budgets are delegated to faculties or departments for them to administer in conformity with the corporate plan. As IT has achieved commodity status, we find both hardware and software being purchased from a variety of budget areas, rather than forming a distinct area for financial resource allocation and expenditure.

Once budgets have been devolved in this way, it becomes difficult to take a strategic view of IT, as the separate budgets across the organisation may be used in inconsistent manners. Technology change has militated against the maintenance of a strong central computing operation, and reporting routes are linked to financial monitoring of the separate budgets. The Central Computing Service may be assigned a role of monitoring expenditures to ensure value for money for orders, but this assumes that expenditure decisions have already been made.

How can this position be retrieved? The approach adopted at Kingston Business School has been to establish an IT Strategy Committee, with the role of considering IT strategy for the ever-larger communities of the Business School, the Faculty of Business and Law, and the Kingston Hill campus. The Committee does not have executive power, but is able to discuss current and future developments in a manner intended to broaden the base of awareness and involvement, making recommendations to the Dean. Membership includes staff and student representation from the different academic schools of the Faculty, the University Computing Service, Library and Audio-Visual Service. A critical role is played by the team of technician-demonstrators, led by the Faculty Technical Officer.

Our IT Strategy Committee is in line with the recommendations of strategists such as Rosabeth Moss Kanter, who have argued the case for alternative structures to facilitate change. She argues, in *The Change Masters* [Kanter 1983]:

"An innovating organisation needs at least two organisations, two ways of arranging and using its people. It needs a hierarchy with specified tasks and functional groupings for carrying out what it already knows how to do, that it can anticipate will be the same in the future. But it also needs a set of flexible vehicles for figuring out how to do what it does not yet know: for encouraging entrepreneurs and engaging the grass roots as well as the elite in the mastery of innovation and change." (p. 205)

Who Needs to Know What?

The purpose of the IT Strategy Committee is to extend awareness of the technology of the site, and the range of expertise available. With changing technology, expertise can come from a number of directions, some of them perhaps unexpected. In a Business School, for example, all staff and students will be regular IT users. Knowledge of the hardware is not sufficient to provide support for users in context: use of business software requires a degree of business knowledge.

When all is going well, access to advice and information may seem relatively casual. However, as the organisational culture becomes more dependent on the use of IT for its normal operations, the issue of disaster prevention assumes critical importance. Procedures are required, to be published, understood and updated in the light of experience. At the heart of the procedures is a process of structured reflection.

Kauffels has considered the problems of managing networks in his *Network Management: Problems, Standards and Strategies* [Kauffels 1992]. He has noted the reappearance of problems of system management:

> "*The individualisation of data processing over recent years has meant that terms such as methodicalness, comprehensibility and integrity have disappeared from the minds of those in responsibility and their staff until, that is, the first data catastrophes and virus show-downs become public.*" (p. 9)

Many organisations had been lulled into a false sense of security, failing to adjust management structures to accommodate changing technology:

> "*The deficiency clearly lies in the form of the organisation and of the corresponding decision-taking hierarchy which are simply not linked to the application of new technologies.*" (p. 10)

There is no alternative to a foundation of technical skill, if an organisation is to withstand crises:

> "*Only appropriate individual know-how guarantees a fast reaction in case of error and long-term secure operation of the network.*" (p. 83)

Technical responsibility cannot simply be delegated to specialists. Everybody involved in managing or using IT must be aware of his or her responsibilities for their own resources, and those for which they are responsible, including data, backing-up requirements and the effect that their actions, or lack of actions, may have on others.

The Kingston Business School technical support team have concluded that the following issues should be addressed by all IT users, and their managers.

ESSENTIAL INFORMATION

Inventory

Hardware

We need to consider which are the key hardware components whose failure or absence would cause most disruption. The file server is a key component in any networked system other than peer-to-peer. If that component fails, then for the time that it is out of action applications are unavailable, shared resources are idle, mail is not sent, and shared data are locked up. For a University, Faculty administration comes to a halt, and students cannot use the systems to do their course work: at worst, examinations are stopped. The failure of some other component, such as a router, a section of cabling, or a print server, might bring some of these problems to some users. Failure of a file server brings them all to everyone who depends on that server.

It is not enough to buy a supposedly reliable machine from a supposedly reliable manufacturer, and cross your fingers. Even the best file server can fail for one of many reasons; the need is to ensure that none of these causes has a catastrophic result.

The server must be up to the job, with room for expansion; enough memory to cope comfortably with current service loads, and room for the addition of further services without significant loss of performance or the threat of system overload. There must be enough disk space to cope with likely data and software expansion: growing databases, electronic mail boxes, busy tape spoolers.

Managers must protect against component failure, and especially against the most common form of disastrous "crash", disk drive failure. There are different levels of protection for your organisation's potential Achilles heel.

At the lowest level, can you, or your supplier, carry a spare hard disk that can be slotted into place within minutes of a major failure, and at worst within hours? This is the minimum requirement, applicable only to non-critical systems.

Today's purpose-built servers come with a number of more sophisticated options that allow, at a cost, increasing levels of fault tolerance resilience and speed of recovery. These include disk mirroring, data guarding and distributed data guarding, and server mirroring. Combined with the capacity to "hot swap" drives, these options offer a very high level of fault tolerance indeed, the trade-off being storage capacity and cost. Disk storage capacity, for instance, will vary from 100% with zero fault tolerance to 50% with disk mirroring; using various levels of data guarding and depending on the number of disk drives used, capacities from 66% to more than 90% can be achieved. A combination of server mirroring and data guarding with hot-swappable drives offers a very high level of system fault tolerance and data integrity.

Ancillaries

Whatever confidence network managers might have in the resilience of their main file servers, this can be no excuse for not providing adequate backup based on tape or disk and using specialised backup software.

By using a Netware utility such as "ncopy" it is possible to make a close copy of a Netware drive, but anyone who has tried to restore a file server from such a copy will soon tell you that it is not up to the job. The most serious failings are that ncopy does not copy the bindery or trustees information, nor does it copy hidden files or files that are open (which means that the system supervisor either has to throw everybody off the network and close down all printers in order to ncopy, or has to come into work at midnight).

There is no substitute for using purpose-built backup software, such as

Netware's own SBACKUP, or any of the many tape backup suites available from third-party software houses. The minimum requirements for such software are that it must be able to back up and restore a server bindery and trustee structure; allow differential backup and restore; back up workstations attached to the network; allow timed backups, i.e. backups that run at midnight on a Saturday night on the assumption that no sane user will be logged into the network at that hour.

Using tape backup systems requires that a good copy be kept of the backup log. In normal running the original log directory is kept in a server system partition; if that should be lost a copy of the log will be needed to safely run the tape restore. Safe keeping of tapes should also be an issue: prudent administrators, and insurance companies, insist that they be kept off-site. There is also the important question of where the tape unit is located: put your tape unit in the server and you get the best of options; but if that server goes down, or worse, is stolen, you are left stranded.

Cabling Structures

To what extent do cabling systems support routing redundancy and continuity of connection? There will be choices between, for example, thin-wire Ethernet and structured cabling, where the latter offers greater facilities, but at greater expense. New installations can take advantage of the experience of previous generations of cabling, which are themselves now facing removal.

Software

Organisations need to ensure the integrity of their software standards, taking into account systems used by others with whom they have regular electronic dealings. Apart from the standards of software for internal use, there are issues of importing and exporting files from other applications and systems.

The advent of the PC brought the Tower of Babel into the realm of software, with the potential for everyone's favourite language to fight to be heard. One advantage of having to teach students is that this tendency is moderated by the need to retain some degree of consistency in the teaching environment. Once software is being delivered centrally, from single networked copies, rational standards become imperative. The advantages in ease of installation, maintenance and support are clear. So are the disadvantages associated with producing upgraded versions of software that is not entirely up-down compatible; and the problems of software that is badly, or incorrectly, configured, or that breaks at a crucial moment for a critical application. Are all operating systems updated and in phase? This will involve checking the terms of licences, and the capacities of workstations used by individual users in the organisation, ensuring that major groups are not excluded from participation.

Is the standard software reliable? Technical support staff will need to monitor reports of the performance of systems on other sites, and resist the blandishments of vendors to continue updating to new and untried versions.

What safeguards are in place against the introduction of incompatible non-standard software? This may be a tricky personnel management issue, as people develop an adherence to applications that they have used in previous organisations, or that they use at home. If the non-standard software allows importing and exporting of files to and from the preferred local standard, then there need be no problem. Incompatible systems, on the other hand, can cause mounting problems the more they are used.

Is antivirus protection in place and up to date? Does it work? A technical support team needs training both in dealing with the problem at a software level and in counselling non-technical users. It is a matter of computer health education.

How quickly can corrupted key software be replaced? It is important that users are able to keep matters in perspective: if problems, once identified, can be dealt with rapidly, the crisis does not have to become disaster.

Location

The majority of network users have no interest in the physical location of any component beyond their own networked PC and the networked printers that they are authorised to use.

Technical support staff, on the other hand, need to know where every component is; how to get to it; and who owns it, or can fix it in the event of failure. Up-to-date physical and logical drawings are essential, with suitable annotation. Particularly important is the cabling diagram, as tracing and fixing cabling faults is often the most common repair activity of network technicians. An especially dangerous time is when staff change locations; cables become detached (accidentally or thoughtlessly); if technicians have been warned in advance of such moves, they can be on the spot to oversee the relocation of equipment, or to alert the movers to what they can and cannot safely disconnect. Equally important is knowledge and authority to access components that might otherwise be locked away, whether in dedicated rooms or cupboards, or in staff offices that are otherwise locked to all but the regular occupier.

Are physical locations of key systems clearly known to key staff? This issue is particularly critical when new staff join, and induction needs to include detailed and formal briefing.

Are these locations secure from accidental damage, weather, vandalism, theft? From experience we argue against complacency: thieves can be persistent and ingenious once they have decided what they want to take.

How accessible are they: to key staff, to key technical staff, to unauthorised personnel? Here we encounter difficult management decisions involving trade-offs between security and accessibility. Technical staff may need advice and support at times of pressure.

Are all logical structures clearly documented? Is that documentation safely lodged with those who can make use of it, safely away from the site?

How readily can physical and logical locations be altered without disruption to the systems? This implies a clear control over physical locations and movement, and excludes the possibility of network users being free to move themselves and their equipment at will.

Access

What access controls are needed and in place? Is there consistency between different facilities in the same organisation? Are these controls sufficient to give protection without unacceptable inhibition of access? How are conflicts resolved?

How is physical access controlled? Is it preferable to use keys, with problems of types and control of copies; or coded locking systems, raising questions of how codes are allocated, and the dangers of code-sharing; or finally, swipe cards?

Do passwords meet agreed standards of security: minimum length, alpha-numeric, frequently changed, not shared? Are there time controls on access? How is this type of control imposed?

Can site security personnel readily gain access in case of emergency?

Owner

Is it clear who owns each item of hardware, software and data? This raises issues of ownership as legal title, or ownership as use and responsibility. It may be vital to resolve these questions for commercial reasons.

Within an organisation there may be interdepartmental ownership conflicts, with implications for budgets and management control. In general, there can be areas of tension between accountants and managers.

User

Who is authorised to use what component of the network? Users need to know what they are allowed to do. How is access to be controlled? It helps if the user can understand the principles behind control of access, to reduce adverse re-actions when access is denied.

How is responsibility distributed between owners and users? This may raise whole new challenges for managers, in businesses and educational institutions, as responsibility for support, maintenance and the performance of particular systems may be critical.

Source

Are there adequate and accessible records of the source of all items of hardware, software and security systems? Are these held in a secure location off-site? Records need to include who sourced each item; from which department; from which external supplier; when; at what price.

What procedures are in place for monitoring and changing sources of supply: price, quality, support? Is procurement seen as an organisational or depart-mental responsibility, and what are the approved procedures?

Support

What day-to-day support is available; in-house or external? Is training of in-house support personnel adequate to meet emergency needs?

Methods

Routine Operation

Are routine operations adequately documented? Is this done in a consistent manner? Are responsibilities clearly allocated and backed up in case of scheduled and unscheduled absence? Does this mean that holiday times are now determined by technical considerations?

Are clear records kept of what has been done, by whom and when? Are these records clearly accessible?

Maintenance

Is routine preventive maintenance in place? How does it work? Is repair maintenance adequate? Does it have an early-warning component?

Replacement

How are malfunctioning items replaced? To what extent can this be done without interruption to services? Have the team practised such operations?

New Processes

What methods are used to monitor and assess new developments in hardware, network and software systems? What external contacts and network connections are used? How are decisions to introduce new systems made? Is this an organisational or local issue?

What measures are taken to ensure that, in the event of new systems failing to operate as expected or required, previous systems can be restored? Have the team practised such operations?

ESSENTIAL PEOPLE

Technical Manager

Is there one person at management level who is responsible for managing all technical activities related to network operation, and answerable to the general management? Is this person given responsibility for planning, documenting and operating all methods to do with network management, maintenance and development?

Does this individual have a disaster recovery plan? Is this individual fully covered in case of absence, scheduled or unscheduled? Can she or he be contacted outside normal working hours in case of emergency?

Network Administrators

Are responsibilities clearly defined? Do network administrators have adequate training? Is there more than one within the department, and are they interchangeable?

To what extent does their performance depend on other personnel, particularly on other departments: for instance, to what extent is a LAN administrator dependent on the activities of a WAN manager?

Does each network administrator have a disaster plan? Is it known to other key personnel? Can administrators be readily contacted outside normal working hours?

Technicians

Are their responsibilities clearly defined? Are technicians adequately trained? Are they interchangeable? Do they know what they are expected to do in case of disaster?

Users

Do users have a clear idea of what systems and services are available to them? What documentation and other information is made available to them? Do they have a clear idea of their responsibilities in using these systems and services? How is this checked?

Are users adequately trained in the use and maintenance of the particular parts of the system that they own? How is this delivered?

Crisis and Disaster

What prevents a crisis from becoming a disaster?

- Rapid diagnosis by a qualified person on the spot.
- Prompt action to an understood and accepted plan.
- Availability of key personnel, as above.
- Redundancy: duplication of hardware, power supply, systems, software, routines, personnel, suppliers.
- Early warning and prompt action: regular monitoring of performance, prompt adjustment to aberrations.
- Communication: rapid movement of essential recovery knowledge from where it resides to where it is needed, be this from the head of a person or from an electronic or paper file.

Organisations that have considered the questions above, and have made appropriate financial commitments to the installation and upkeep of their IT systems, will face periodic crises, but these should not have to become disasters.

DISASTER RECOVERY PLANNING

There is only the fight to recover what has been lost
And found and lost again and again: and now, under conditions
That seem unpropitious. But perhaps neither gain nor loss.
For us, there is only the trying. The rest is not our business.

T. S. Eliot (1888–1965), East Coker

Langsford and Moffett [1993], in their *Distributed Systems Management,* have noted the considerable additional burden that has fallen on system managers:

"*Freeing the users from the burden of organising, monitoring and controlling the environment has resulted in a shift of this responsibility on to the distributed systems support and to the system's operators and managers.*" *(p. 2)*

System managers may be obliged to curtail the extent of individual decision-making when it affects the shared system, as autonomous decision-making in different parts of the organisation may hinder coordinated planning.

The nature of the management task has changed, as system management has to take cognisance of the strategic objectives of the organisation, thus bringing together previously separate management functions:

"*Whereas the business manager's staff (identifying the need) and the IT manager (identifying the system to meet the need) could readily be distinguished from each other when the technical solution proposed was to provide a mainframe computer, the 'downsizing' introduced by distributed processing is drawing these two categories into the same type of person.*" *(p. 55)*

Once the common interests have been identified, the time has come for disaster recovery planning. There needs to be a disaster planning policy that requires each system to be considered for its criticality and defines how any critical system is to be recovered. It should define what is the maximum recovery time, and how all data, communications and processors are to be backed up to enable rapid recovery in the event of any conceivable disaster.

One way of reducing the likelihood of disasters is to plan for them. The role of disaster recovery planning is to ensure that:

- The effects of theft, fire, flood and electrical power loss are taken into consideration in determining the location of master and slave hardware and software.
- Enough of the resources above are installed, maintained and available when needed.
- Efficient communications procedures are adopted and maintained to inform people of changes and developments that may affect their method of work and backing up.
- There exist adequate alternative resources that can cope, at least in the short term, in providing an effective, albeit reduced, service until normal

working can be resumed.

- Normal working is restored in the shortest possible time through effective insurance cover, and a contingency fund that will have been set up by management; in the event of this being used, it must be re-established without delay, in case of a further disaster following.

Disaster recovery planning can be seen as having three separately identifiable roles in the organisation:

- Preparation: all staff must be aware of their roles and responsibilities in case of disaster.
- Simulation: plans can be tested by simulating disaster situations, and monitoring responses.
- Training: corporate training programmes should now incorporate disaster recovery, including reflection on the insights provided into the importance of different functions and post-holders for the survival of the organisation.

Fisher [1994], in his *Information Systems Security*, has noted the dangers of relying on the "quick fix". He emphasises the importance of a disaster recovery plan:

"All organisations should have an up-to-date, tested, organisational disaster recovery plan. The end product, first and foremost, is not a paper document but a tested, proven capability to recover. Testing is the vehicle that changes disaster recovery planning from a concept into a reality." (p. 13)

System designers are seen as having additional obligations to users:

"The designer has an obligation to educate the user as to the benefits of all data security safeguards." (p. 75)

PREVENTING IT DISASTERS AT KINGSTON BUSINESS SCHOOL

Kingston Business School is responding to this challenge, with a planning approach aimed at maximum involvement of users.

Background

The Faculty of Business places great reliance on its networked computer system. Recent history has shown that, although the crises we have encountered have been minimised through the skill, resolve and commitment of the technical team, a planned prevention and recovery strategy is now needed.

Strategy

- PC users, whether stand-alone or networked, should ensure that there are copies of their own data files. This practice is not well maintained throughout the University, although awareness of the requirement is high; implementation tends not to be considered until data loss has already occurred.
- Networks should have their server disk(s) backed up to another medium using a grandfather/father/son method. Backup of networked PC user files could also be stored on this medium, directly or via the server; this should not absolve the PC user of his/her own requirement.
- Whatever backup method is used, the copies should be stored separate from the machine concerned, and in the case of servers/minicomputers/mainframes should preferably be in a fireproof safe.
- Wherever possible, duplication of services should either be extant or capable of being brought back into service within 24 hours. The machines concerned should be separated such that even a major failure of one, caused, for example, by a fire, will not affect the other.
- UPSs (uninterruptable power supplies) must be used in conjunction with all major items of equipment.
- Avoidance, and gradual phasing out, of other single points of failure.
- Members of the technical team will work in shifts, so that at least one member of the team is available throughout the "normal working time" of the Faculty, i.e. from 8.30 a.m. to 9.30 p.m. each weekday during term time.
- The technical staff of the Faculty will undergo continuous on-the-job training, in order to ensure that, in the event of a crisis, the risks of a disaster are minimised in the shortest possible time.
- Each member of the team will be responsible for "shadowing" another critical member, in order to cover for planned and unplanned absences.
- A contingency fund will be set up from the start of each fiscal period, of sufficient size to cope with any foreseeable occurrence. This will need to be replenished without excessive delay in the event of it being used, to ensure that a further loss does not cripple the systems.

Prevention

- A Netbuilder "ring", triangulating the key areas of the campus, will be installed, in order to cope with a fault in the "backbone" cabling structure or routing equipment. Fibre-optic links are already in place between the main Business School buildings and the Computer Centre, and from the Computer Centre to the mid-level building.
- Through the purchase of a second DAT drive for use in the server Socrates, matching that already in use in the server Galileo, resilience in backup swaps will be achieved.

- Additional hard disk drives for the two matching servers will need to be ordered, so that mirroring of each server can be achieved across the network. This will result in a no-loss situation, in the event of a major breakdown of either server.

Responsibilities

In order to maintain a continuum of the strategy outline, new job titles will be used for the Faculty team, delineating the responsibilities of the post with regard to disaster prevention and recovery. The responsibilities outlined will form part of the full job description, as currently in force.

- *Faculty Technical Manager:* Responsible for ensuring adherence to the strategy, implementation, testing of its effectiveness and its modification where necessary.
- *PC Network Manager:* Responsible for the day-to-day running of the PC networks, and the first call in the event of a crisis in that system. Will take on the FTM role in his/her absence, for the purposes of safeguarding the network strategy.
- *Deputy PC Network Manager:* Will shadow the PC Network Manager, ensuring that continued working can be maintained during periods of absence. This to include holidays, sickness and lunchtime cover.
- *SUN Network Manager:* Responsible for the day-to-day running of the SUN network, and the first call in the event of a crisis in that system.
- *Deputy SUN Network Manager:* Will shadow the SUN Network Manager, ensuring that continued working can be maintained during periods of absence. This to include holidays, sickness and lunchtime cover.
- *Infrastructure Technician:* To be a trained trouble-shooter in network cabling systems, capable of diagnosis and repair of faults in the thin-wire and structured cabling systems.
- *Junior Technician:* Will shadow the Infrastructure Technician, ensuring that continued working can be maintained during periods of absence. This to include holidays, sickness and lunchtime cover.

Responsibilities

Responsibilities apply from the top down. Senior management must instigate a professional approach to ensuring that the IT management is as coherent as, and is seen to be as important as, the other departments of the organisation, such as finance, personnel, etc.

- *Management:* In knowing the likely costs of crisis and disasters, and in providing appropriate budgets to enable prevention and rapid recovery.
- *Senior Technical Manager:* In facilitating management knowledge, in training and supporting technical staff, and in preparing and maintaining an adequate disaster recovery plan.
- *Network Administrators:* In establishing and maintaining secure systems.
- *Technical staff:* In providing timely and error-free support.
- *Owners and users:* In exercising care and proper maintenance of hardware and software under their control.

ACCOUNTABILITY

In the modern networked organisation, all personnel work in a technological environment, with a degree of interdependence. All must be held accountable for their actions as users of technology. The organisation must ensure that all users have access to the requisite knowledge and technical support, and that the technical support team have been provided with the necessary resources and facilities to perform their responsibilities. Corporate strategy must include provision for staff development and an ongoing process of technical updating and maintenance.

Pragmatics

Given agreement to the above general principles, some hard issues are left to be resolved by managers who typically work under pressure of time and financial resources.

1. What proportion of annual capital equipment expenditure (in a Higher Education Institution) should be devoted to the following?

   - Insurance
   - Maintenance
   - Infrastructure
   - Furniture
   - Software licences
   - Security
   - Teaching equipment
   - Administration
   - Staff needs for teaching
   - Staff needs for research
   - Student needs

2. What has to be cut when costs are controlled?

- Levels of available technology
- Non-standard systems
- Numbers of users
- Numbers of software licences
- Training and support
- Information services

3. Given a new set of constraints on managers:

- Cash-limited budgets
- Increased exposure through networking
- *De facto* standardisation of technology
- A developed resale market for stolen computer equipment
- Raised general awareness of IT

How can increased funds be allocated to security and disaster prevention out of a diminishing budget?

4. Given:

- The fragility of the insurance market
- The declining cost of IT hardware
- Rapidity of obsolescence
- Standardisation and interchangeability
- Maintenance charges by vendors
- Frequency of upgrading and version changes

What is the responsible attitude to take to insurance and maintenance?

5. When purchasing equipment:

- Is it worth taking out maintenance and insurance on all items?
- What should be the approach to "bundled" software, provided "free of charge"?
- What is the case for and against using public-domain and shareware software?

6. Given the objective of managing an open facility:

- To what extent should system functionality be reduced in the cause of security?
- How far can network structures be segmented and protected to prevent inappropriate leakages of confidential information?
- How can sensible backup procedures be introduced and policed in a networked environment?
- How can managers cope with the impossibility of foolproof virus detection systems?

Information Technology and Business Ethics: Case Studies

7

> This is the excellent foppery of the world, that, when we are sick in fortune,
> often the surfeit of our own behaviour, we make guilty of our own disasters
> the sun, the moon, and the stars; as if we were villains by necessity, fools by
> heavenly compulsion, knaves, thieves and treachers by spherical predomin-
> ance, drunkards, liars and adulterers by an enforced obedience of planetary
> influence; and all that we are evil in, by a divine thrusting on: an admirable
> evasion of whoremaster man, to lay his goatish disposition to the charge of
> a star!
>
> *Shakespeare, King Lear, Act 1, Scene 2: Edmund*

In a similar way, we often seek to blame our mistakes on the computer. There is
an ethical dimension to IT disasters, as attempts are made to shift responsibility
from men to machines. The excuse of ignorance of IT wears thin when offered by
those with senior management positions.

The debate has been limited, for it would involve a new combination of the
professional ethics of IT professionals and the business ethics of the manager. In
neither case does professional status absolve the individual from his or her
responsibilities as a citizen and member of the privileged educated elite.

Information technology, like all technology, is entirely value-laden. It must be
seen as a process in which values have shaped the creation, design and application of the device, product or service. Technological decisions must be recognised for what they are: moral decisions.

There are now a number of different cases worthy of consideration, across the
full range of modern business.

Wessex Regional Health Authority

INTRODUCTION

The management and information systems in this large Regional Health Authority have come to recent public prominence, with hearings by the Public Accounts Committee of the House of Commons, and a detailed television documentary. The case should be seen in the context of Government reforms of the National Health Service, and the introduction of more commercial practices. This has meant cultural conflict problems for Health Service administrators, accustomed to public-sector modes of working but obliged to deal with private-sector consultants and contractors.

Another complicating factor has been the development of multi-disciplinary management consultancies, the new civil service, as they undertake advisory work previously the province of public-sector professionals, but also contractors keen to tender for work for public bodies. The best-known consultancies have taken on curious hybrid roles, which may involve parts of the organisations in tendering for public business managed by other parts of the same organisation, raising issues of "Chinese Walls", better known for their reported erection in the City of London following "Big Bang".

IT vendors have also acquired an ambiguous status. IBM UK, for example, is a major employer in the UK, and has seconded senior staff to a number of key public-sector positions, including Government Chief Scientific Advisers. Such individuals remain on the IBM payroll while advising Ministers on national policy.

Within this context, business and IT professionals have been obliged to develop their own *modus operandi*. They would arguably have benefited from external advice or a public regime of explicit statements of interests, rather than being content to rely on unvoiced assumptions.

The fundamental problem in this complex situation has been one of accountability. In the former National Health Service, the Regional Health Authority included a large proportion of democratically elected representatives. These have been replaced by business nominees, many of whom have commercial interests relating to the work of the Health Authority. Senior industrialists have been seconded to executive positions; management consultants have both developed forward strategies and then sought contracts for implementation.

It was an attractive idea to develop a single information system to link the different hospitals, services and units across a region: if the system succeeded it could serve as a model for other regions, with considerable commercial benefits for the partners. Budgets and timescales were conditioned by this objective, imposing pressure on individual professionals to support the project and avoid action that might be prejudicial to its success.

In the cold light of day, or in the dispassionate account of a television documentary, the project seems fatally flawed. Strategic managers appear to have had little idea of the technical complexity of the task to which they were committed, and gave short shrift to those who recommended caution. The outcome was a working system in only one small part of the region, and national questions about the costs incurred: money allocated for the National Health Service had been used to pay consultants and vendors, many of whom had also acted as advisers for the Authority. The CCTA are now considering new procedures.

ETHICAL QUESTIONS

- Should IT professionals participate in projects that they believe to be infeasible?
- Should management consultants be allowed to bid for contracts under strategies and programmes that they have designed as Government advisers?
- To whom can professionals turn when they are concerned about malpractice and maladministration?
- Can a code of practice be developed to cover insider knowledge in public organisations?
- How can professionals be made accountable to the public, on whose behalf they are supposedly working?
- Who is held responsible when information systems fail to perform according to specification?
- How can professionals be advised on appropriate practices in this new hybrid environment?

Compliance with Financial Services Legislation

INTRODUCTION

The Financial Services Act of 1985 deregulated the financial institutions of the City of London, allowing many institutions to diversify into new services, previously the province of separate professionals. Building Societies, for example, took the opportunity to become Banks, and took over large chains of estate agents to integrate their housing activities. Stockbrokers entered the unfamiliar world of market-making. Merchant Banks expanded their range of services.

Many financial institutions found that they got out of their depth when they ventured away from familiar activities. Building Societies and Insurance

Companies have been disposing of their estate agencies in the wake of the collapse of the housing market. The number of market-makers has contracted. Many Merchant Banks have become vulnerable to take-over, or fallen into foreign ownership.

Behind the headlines of the rise and fall of the City lies a series of predicaments for business and IT professionals. Reporting to senior management, their role has been to deliver on corporate objectives in an unregulated market. Responsibility for performance has been devolved to the individual or small group, with accountability seen in purely financial terms.

The insurance industry has encountered particular problems, with both the collapse of the Lloyds market in light of several successive years of losses, and the exposure of widespread inadequacies in the sale of personal pension schemes to public-sector employees. In each case industry insiders are alleged to have made large profits at the expense of the less informed investor.

In theory, there are a set of regulatory bodies whose job it is to root out malpractice. However, as long as they are based on self-regulation and the public agencies such as the Serious Fraud Office are held up for ridicule following the collapse of publicised cases, there is an absence of serious enforcement of standards.

Business and IT come together in this controversial area. Just as IT is a vital tool in high-speed financial dealing on international currency markets, so it also provides the means by which such dealings can be monitored. The collapse of the Stock Market paperless TAURUS system has exposed the fragility of the grasp of senior management on the technological environment in which they work. The Securities and Investment Authority has been considering options for transaction monitoring with the support of IT, but has no system in place, and no firm recommendations.

We are left, as a result of frailty in both business and IT, with a curious legal, and therefore ethical, dilemma. In practice, the City of London operates on the basis that compliance with financial services legislation equates with failure to be prosecuted for infringements. The role of lawyers has become one of advising clients how to organise their affairs such that they are not open to allegations of infringement. The law is used defensively, rather than proactively.

ETHICAL QUESTIONS

- Is it correct to describe financial fraud as a victimless crime?
- How should professionals respond when they become aware of possible illegality in their organisation?
- What are the limits beyond which a financial services professional should not make use of her specialist knowledge?
- How can insider dealing be defined in the days of IT and knowledge-based systems?

- Who is responsible for failures of information systems in financial services organisations?
- What professional structures are necessary in financial services?
- To what extent is the ethical position of lawyers compromised?
- How do auditors deal with malpractice in client companies?

Training and Enterprise Councils

INTRODUCTION

Training and Enterprise Councils are officially private-sector companies, but they were established under Government policy and are responsible for the expenditure of public money in the geographical areas where they are the designated authority. Council members are drawn from senior local businessmen, with many staff formerly Civil Servants in the Department of Employment.

In the past a large proportion of training by the employed workforce was acquired through an extended process of apprenticeship regulated by Industrial Training Boards. The Government first abolished Industrial Training Boards, establishing the Manpower Services Commission to lead national initiatives. They then removed trade unions from influence on training, establishing the Training Commission. The establishment of the Training Agency distanced delivery of training from Government, and the network of 82 Training and Enterprise Councils across the country, supposedly led by local captains of industry, was hailed as demonstrating a welcome increased involvement from the private sector.

The Department of Employment is concerned with the reduction of unemployment, and officers are set targets for reductions in their areas of responsibility. Training initiatives by TECs are primarily concerned with reduction of unemployment figures, and resources have been relocated from long-term education to short-term schemes. Little attention has been given to upgrading the skills of those in work, and the initial purpose of National Vocational Qualifications was to accredit existing skills and competence, rather than to provide additional training. The same budgets are recycled to initiate successive schemes, maintaining the appearance of activity while public-sector expenditure is being reduced.

This situation poses dilemmas for business and IT professionals. Public perceptions of training will differ from current practice. Training organisations depend for their existence on success in bidding for public funds, presenting information tailored to demonstrate their organisation's compliance with Government requirements and commitment to achieve Government objectives. Contracts are typically determined at short notice, with a period of frenzied activity at the end of the financial year, but the official position is of continuity and coherence.

National Vocational Qualifications have an important part to play, as they provide an index of the effectiveness of a TEC. A proportion of TEC funding is linked to the number of NVQs awarded in their programmes: payment by results, so it is important to avoid failure. Back to basic Victorian values and methods indeed. TECs are officially seen as in competition in the training "market", but it is a market created and controlled by Government policy.

ETHICAL QUESTIONS

- Can professionals assemble and present statistics and reports without regard to the content and implications?
- Does it make a difference whether one is working for a public- or private-sector organisation?
- Is it ethical to be "economical with the truth" in the area of employment and unemployment?
- Why cannot information be shared between those working for shared objectives of training and the reduction of unemployment?
- Is it appropriate for training programmes be run on a profit basis while using public money?
- Is it acceptable for companies to improve their own financial position by shedding workers, while they are reluctant to contribute to programmes to reduce unemployment?
- Is it ethical to purport to offer training for jobs when no jobs are available?

Selling Solutions

INTRODUCTION

"Executive information system" is the name of a solution, rather than the description of a system. Such is the power of language that vendors have sought to sell solutions rather than getting involved in the details of the human systems in which problems have to be solved.

Just as "expert systems" was a popular label to apply to products, and "user-friendly" was a required characteristic, executive information systems have been provided as the answer to company problems. The companies with the problems were often software vendors, seeking to rebadge old products.

The claim of EIS is that all executives can become confident IT users, with tools meeting their personal information and decision support needs. This claim warrants close scrutiny by business information technology prospective professionals, for it embodies a series of critical assumptions regarding IT use and executive decisions, and of the working of organisations.

Where EIS vendors are challenged on these issues, they typically respond that they are producing tools for others to use. When pushed, they concede that they do not use their own products to help run their own companies. They accept that EIS is the flavour of the moment, but that their future emphasis is more likely to be on networking and groupwork, using technology to support a different model of decision-making and organisation.

The typical EIS is designed to enable an executive to take a more active role in financial monitoring and control. The screen display will highlight figures that may cause concern, and may allow the executive to "drill down" to investigate the area of the business that appears to be in trouble. Few executives take full advantage of such facilities, and may be as happy with the traditional briefing book service. More seriously, it may be thought that an EIS encourages "driving using the rear mirror", letting business decisions be determined by past financial results within a narrow focus of reference.

EIS highlights the role of the executive as financial controller at a time when many would argue that the needs of business require innovative decisions, particularly in the field of manufacturing. Information is reduced to figures, and complete information is assumed. Reporting lines are assumed to be vertical, with the executive entitled to drill down before reporting up to her manager.

A number of vendors have been caught out by the pace of technological change, and are attempting to extend the life of existing products by rebadging as EIS systems. They are further challenged by changes in operating systems and user interfaces, whereby a number of expensive features of EIS systems are now provided routinely under Windows. Open Systems and interoperability of operating systems pose further problems. The EIS dinosaur, with expensive licence and maintenance costs, may have had its day. The consultant using customised versions of the same technology will doubtless linger on, so many vendors have switched their emphasis to management consultancy.

ETHICAL QUESTIONS

- Is it responsible professional practice to provide an executive with a tool he or she does not understand and whose limits have not been explained?
- Where does the responsibility lie when faulty decisions are made with the aid of a computer system, such as an EIS?
- To what extent are the executive's decisions affected by the model of the organisation embodied in the EIS?
- Should decisions for the future be dominated by consideration of financial performance in the past?
- Will the nature of management change by virtue of the introduction of new software approaches?

- To what extent is a professional obliged to understand the strengths and limitations of the tools of the trade?
- When the management consultancy introduces an EIS for a client, where does the effective control lie?

Defence and Diversification

INTRODUCTION

There are a number of common problems internationally, in leading nations of both West and East. During the years of the Cold War, considerable efforts were put into defence, which consumed a large proportion of research funding and resources, and distorted the workings of the market in skills and technology. Since the fall of the Berlin Wall it has proved difficult to divert energies from defence to civil production, and to diversify the activities of defence companies.

Information technology is a focus of attention as a generic technology capable of both defence and civil applications. New-generation computing projects, developing high-performance parallel architectures with artificial intelligence and speech input, have sought to address both sectors, but have fallen foul of the different prevailing cultures. Defence electronics has been concerned with high-specification, high-cost, low-quantity products, with a single principal purchaser at national or alliance level. Civil electronics, by contrast, has had to deal with challenges of appropriate specification, low cost, mass production and a multiplicity of customers in an international fast-moving market. The disciplines of the two cultures are not the same.

Technology-based industries depend on the skills of the workforce and its management by executives who can plan for and adjust to future conditions. The defence industries provided an environment where companies could respond to Government programmes, and work on a cost-plus basis whereby their research and development costs were met by Government. Research and development were conducted in an environment of both official secrecy and commercial confidentiality, and it was relatively rare for inventions and processes of military origin to be transferred into civil use. The record was somewhat different in the United States, where State aid to industry was usually in the form of Pentagon contracts, meaning that firms such as Boeing, Ford and General Motors had development costs of civil products funded from military contracts.

Prior to the end of the Cold War there were a number of collaborative programmes with Government support, part of whose motivation was to aid the process of technology transfer from defence to civil production. The Alvey Programme in Advanced Information Technology was one such in Britain, mirrored by the European ESPRIT Programme and the Japanese Fifth Generation Programme, as well as by initiatives in the USA. Companies with experience of fully funded military work found it hard to engage in part-funded civil collaborations, and to work with University research groups. The British Government refused funding for a continuation of the Alvey Programme after the initial budget was exhausted in 1986. The ESPRIT Programme continues, and the Japanese have moved on to further pre-competitive collaborative projects. The US Government is now supporting initiatives, involving major defence contractors, to develop a new generation of fuel-efficient and non-polluting cars.

Recent years in Britain have seen a collapse in the defence industries, and a failure to diversify to successful civil work. The advice from GEC to British Aerospace has been to "stick to the knitting" after a period of diversification into automobiles, property and construction. Thousands of jobs have been lost, and areas of technological expertise closed down. The British Aerospace Kingston factory has been bulldozed, cleared to make way for housing.

Amid the turmoil of industrial change, the stated view of Government has been that market forces must prevail. For defence industries the Government, as near-monopoly customer, dictates the market. As defence orders contract, and are not replaced by civil initiatives, the market is destroyed. The strategic consequences for British industry are serious, and were the basis for the resignation of the President of the Board of Trade from his post as Secretary of State for Defence in 1986.

Individual professionals are left in an invidious position. They went into defence electronics to serve the country and meet intellectual challenges. With the end of the Cold War, the country appears to care little about industry, technology or intellectual challenge.

ETHICAL QUESTIONS

- Government is encouraging defence suppliers to work for overseas contractors, including Japan and Germany. What problems does this pose to professionals?
- Did dependence on military contracts featherbed British contractors and prevent them from meeting the challenges of the market? Who gained and lost from the process?
- Is it ethical for retiring Civil Servants to join the Boards of defence companies, and for defence contractors to be seconded to Government?
- How can defence industry habits of secrecy and confidentiality be changed to meet the needs of the civil market-place?
- How can habits of collaboration be developed in a competitive world with a legacy of Cold War?
- What are the core skills that should be transferred from defence to civil industry, and how can this be done?
- How can the State assist in this process of culture change?
- Can professionals work on a project without concern for its objectives and the intended use of its products?
- What happens to whistle-blowers in the defence and civil sectors?

Marketing Quality

INTRODUCTION

Marketing is about educating and conditioning customer perceptions, and quality is a characteristic of products and processes likely to make them more appealing to customers. In a world of finite varieties in actual products and processes, perceptions can be all-important.

The business and IT professional may be in a position to know the difference between the truth as he sees it about his company's product or process, and the accepted public perception. He may be employed to ensure that the two stay separate.

Quality as defined by BSI and ISO tends to refer to organisational procedures, and the extent to which they conform to their stated objectives and documented procedures. Quality certification thus denotes consistency relative to the company's own standards, rather than any objective rating.

Professionals and procedures may thus be used to mislead, and may be aided by specialist public-relations consultants who customise their descriptions to the requirements of the consumer.

The business and IT professional will encounter difficulty if she does not understand the situation she is in. Systems will have to be designed to produce the result most appropriate for the consumer, presenting a benign interface. At some stage the system will need to relate to the real world or a model thereof, and the system designer will have to be aware of the point when modelling becomes marketing.

New-generation marketing professionals make great play of the use of IT in marketing, with EDI (Electronic Data Interchange), EPOS (Electronic Point of Sale) and EFTPOS (Electronic Funds Transfer at Point of Sale) opening new opportunities for information processing in the cause of enhanced sales. As marketing becomes more quantitative, it can become more settled in the ideological role of conditioning the consumer to purchase the desired product.

ETHICAL QUESTIONS

- Should marketing professionals be subject to ethical codes?
- What are the implications for privacy for EPOS and EFTPOS?
- How can the confusions over quality be untangled?
- How should quality standards be applied to software, and with what implications for responsibility?
- What are the limits of marketing in a free-market economy?
- Is the IT professional reduced to the role of mercenary when working in marketing?

Talking to Your Computer

INTRODUCTION

Until recently the idea of a speech-driven computer was restricted to the realms of science fiction. During the Alvey Programme there was extensive work on a speech-driven workstation incorporating highly parallel computer architecture, and complex computational linguistics work in speech comprehension. There was particular motivation for work in this field in Japan, where the complexities of their traditional script prevented them from taking full advantage of word processing systems, and it was clearly preferable to be able to talk to the computer.

We now find commercial products reaching the market, linked to industry-standard personal computers. Less ambitious than the research projects of the 1980s, the current systems concentrate on matching the patterns of particular utterances with those of a database of words. The outcome is a speech interface to standard software, with the potential for speech macros tailored to the needs of particular users.

The technology has been shown to work, but a group project of final-year Business Information Technology students at Kingston Business School is concerned with the business context of use. They are working with Shakespeare Speechwriters Ltd, and developing case studies with users of the system.

ETHICAL QUESTIONS

- Who is likely to use such systems, for what purpose and with what consequences for the work of the business?
- If the system is used instead of dictating to a secretary, what are the implications for the secretary?
- How will the operations of, for example, telephone sales departments be affected?
- How should such technology be introduced, with what training, and with what impact on systems development in the organisation?
- Who should determine what new technologies are introduced into an organisation?
- What should happen to those whose jobs are displaced by new technology?
- How should the marketing claims of new technology innovations be monitored and controlled?
- How should the technology be made available to those whose need is greatest, but whose market power is limited?

Arms, Technology and Business Ethics

Issues involving arms and technology raise ethical problems in themselves, and the consequences of mismanagement can be disastrous on an international scale. These problems are compounded when they are considered in the context of the complexity of Government policy and international affairs. What appear on the surface to be straightforward questions involving business decisions in the light of market forces may have further dimensions worthy of consideration.

Conclusions that may be drawn from the case studies outlined below include that businessmen need to be aware both of the technical potential of the products in which they deal, and of the political and ethical context within which they are seeking to make money.

ARMS TO IRAQ

The purpose of the British Foreign Office, Ministry of Defence and Intelligence Services is to prevent disasters in the nation's foreign and defence policies. The purpose of the Department of Trade and Industry is to sponsor and promote the interests of the nation's enterprises, including those engaged in exports, whose collapse would be disastrous for the nation's future. In a working democratic system the people are both the shareholders and major stakeholders in Government operations.

Crucial to the court case in which executives of Matrix-Churchill were defendants, and to the subsequent Inquiry by Lord Justice Scott, was the fact that machine tools can be put to a dual use, making machinery for either the military or the civil sector. The same piece of equipment can produce products for both markets, though at any given stage a particular mode of use may be given prominence.

It would appear that Matrix-Churchill was wholly owned by Iraqi interests and existed primarily to equip the Iraqi arms industry during the long Iran–Iraq War. Machine tools were being exported from Britain to build the Supergun, new nuclear weapons and delivery systems for chemical and biological weapons. In order to evade United Nations sanctions, it was deemed prudent for the company to emphasise the dual-use potential of machine tools when seeking export clearance, and for Government to suppress or ignore the evidence from the Intelligence Services regarding the destinations of consignments, either sent direct to Iraq or via Jordan. Given that among the Matrix-Churchill executives were informers for British Intelligence, the importance of continuing the flow of machine tools was seen as justifying protection for the intelligence sources until Customs and Excise insisted on a court case.

The offending equipment was largely destroyed by Allied aircraft and Cruise missiles during the Gulf War and subsequent air strikes.

Matrix-Churchill can be seen as relatively small players in a much larger game, which involved the Western nations first funding the development of Saddam Hussein's war capability and then taking military action against him in the name of the United Nations. Even during the Gulf War hostilities, CIA agents continued to supply arms to Iraq.

A full account of the events can be read in Alan Friedman's *Spider's Web: Bush, Saddam, Thatcher and the Decade of Deceit* [Friedman 1993]. Friedman, who works for the *Financial Times*, has served for many years as a correspondent in Italy and in the United States, and has dramatically illuminated the links between the Matrix-Churchill case and other recent international business scandals. These include the collapse of the Italian-controlled bank BNL in Atlanta having lent $6 billion to Iraq, and the collapse of the computer and defence company Ferranti in Britain after the scandal involving their American subsidiary International Signal and Control (ISC). ISC, led by James Guerin, had been selling cluster bombs to Iraq via the Cardoen company in Chile prior to their collapse and subsequent rescue by Ferranti, who bought ISC without making a thorough examination of the financial books.

The later sections of Friedman's book provide a remarkably up-to-date briefing for observers of the Scott Inquiry, to which the Prime Minister gave evidence in January 1994. Mr Major indicated that as Chief Financial Secretary to the Treasury, as Foreign Secretary, as Chancellor of the Exchequer and as Prime Minister he had not been told what was going on, and had not thought to ask. He indicated that he could not be expected to read, and take responsibility for, details in letters that passed across his desk. Such a position has implications for business ethics.

Subsequent sessions with Cabinet Ministers and senior Civil Servants have unearthed divergent views on ministerial responsibility and the use of Public Interest Immunity Certificates to prevent the disclosure of information that might prove embarrassing to Government.

So What?

The details of the alleged misconduct of Presidents, Prime Ministers and Ministers in this individual case do not concern us here, but there are fundamental issues that are of major importance for a consideration both of the prevention of IT disasters and of business ethics.

Tools

Machine tools are a dual-use technology. So are computer systems. Whatever the intention of the vendor, it is theoretically possible for systems to be put to a radically different use once installed. It is, however, very hard for a high-technology company to switch from supplying predominantly a military market, with one or two principal customers, to meeting the different and more diverse needs of a civil market. This dilemma has been felt by British defence companies, including those working in defence electronics. With the end of the Cold War they have been seeking to diversify, not by moving into civil markets but by selling to new military clients, often in unstable regions. There will be temptations to be lured by market forces beyond the limits of what might be politically advisable.

Policies

Government Ministers have faced conflicting priorities, and sought to prevent a number of different disasters. Clearly no Government wishes to become engaged in war or to arm a potential aggressor, but they may be more worried by a rival power in the same region whose expansion they seek to limit. If they can meet a foreign policy goal by providing business to a British-based company, then this may prevent the disaster of increased unemployment. This was the justification, for example, for linking aid to Malaysia for the construction of the Pergau Dam to major arms contracts for British contractors, in breach of British and international law.

On the other hand, if plans in one area of policy start to go wrong, the implications can be widespread, unpredictable and potentially disastrous for the Government or Governments concerned. Damage limitation becomes the order of the day, in a battle where truth is an early casualty. In the Pergau Dam case, following a Malaysian boycott of British contracts after allegations of impropriety, we also saw links to major financial scandals involving the Hong Kong banking community and international accountancy firms through the trial of George Tam over his company Carrian.

We must always consider international dimensions. In the case of the Iran–Iraq War, there were clearly covert American operations, supported at the highest political levels, intended to arm both sides in the conflict. Britain was under pressure to comply with such schemes.

Personal Ethics

Individuals can find themselves in difficult positions once policies have gone wrong and the public spotlight is applied. We have seen the problems and embarrassments of Ministers and Civil Servants when asked direct questions by a personable and inquisitorial barrister, without the protection of Parliamentary privilege or persiflage.

Friedman, in *Spider's Web*, has cast light on the dilemmas of individuals, less publicly known, who are faced with orders or requests that they find unacceptable, worrying, or personally threatening. During what he describes as a "decade of deceit", ethical issues appear to have received little attention compared with the moves in the political power game on the big stage. Yet all of the actors in the drama were, of course, individuals.

Friedman's book is particularly interesting because it does not, as the reader might have expected, allege a conspiracy involving personal gain. As he concludes, what has become known as Iraqgate:

"Embodies a broader, more systematic abuse of power, one that contributed to the prolonging of the Iran–Iraq War, in which one million people died, and to Operation Desert Storm, which cost the lives of tens of thousands of innocent Iraqis who were already living in the hardship of Saddam's tyranny."

His conclusions can be summarised in extracts from the closing chapter of the book, entitled "Endgame":

"Low-level American, British and Italian footsoldiers in government, in banking, in the military and in the world of espionage ended up taking the fall for the US-driven embrace of Saddam Hussein. In the end these individuals were punished for decisions that were really made at the policy level, and in government-to-government understandings."

"The motivations behind this sorry chapter in international affairs differed from country to country. For London, it was the mercantilist tradition that mattered most."

The truth was suppressed in the cause of business:

"The politicians perceived their actions as reasonable damage control, or as the legitimate desire to protect state secrets. But the absence of malice is no excuse. The result was cover-up, and the cavalier manipulation of truth at the highest level of government."

STAR WARS

I have been struck by the similarities of the issues raised by Iraqgate and by Star Wars, when considered in terms of tools, policies and personal ethics. I explored some of these issues in my *Star Wars: A Question of Initiative* [Ennals 1986], in *Artificial Intelligence and Human Institutions* [Ennals 1991] and in a contribution, "Decoupling research from military applications" [Ennals 1989], to an international conference "Ways Out of the Arms Race". Related issues have been explored by international scientists in the Pugwash Movement, in *Scientists, the Arms Race and Disarmament* [Rotblat 1982], and by defence and artificial intelligence experts at the Swedish International Peace Research Institute, in *Arms and Artificial Intelligence* [Din 1987].

The Star Wars controversy itself provoked a flood of books.

Star Wars and Iraqgate involved the same Government Departments and Ministers in the same countries in the West, with many of the same companies, Civil Servants and individual entrepreneurs. In both cases dual-use technologies were involved, but with companies more accustomed to work in the defence market. In both cases the complexity of policies and events left individuals in difficult ethical positions.

In the case of Star Wars, I chose to act as a "whistle-blower" and dissident campaigner, resigning my research management posts at Imperial College and the Alvey Directorate of the Department of Trade and Industry once a Memorandum of Understanding was signed, in order to continue my opposition to Government policy. My resignation was closely followed by those of the Secretaries of State for Defence (Michael Heseltine) and for Trade and Industry (Leon Brittan), who opposed the policy of participation in Star Wars that was enforced by the Prime Minister, but were obliged to cite other reasons for their departures from the Government.

This interpretation of events was endorsed by Tam Dalyell MP in his book *Misrule* [Dalyell 1987]. He identified the links between the Westland and Star Wars issues in the case of Michael Heseltine:

"What on earth happened between the third week of November and the first week of December 1985 to transform Ministerial indifference into a resigning issue for a senior cabinet Minister?

The real issue must seem at first sight to be irrational. Early in December 1985, another issue had surfaced in acute form, in the highest echelons of the British Government. This was British participation in the American Strategic Defense Initiative programme, popularly but misleadingly dubbed 'Star Wars'. Certainly the substantive decision about, and possibly even the Prime Minister's first public announcement of, British participation in SDI was made without proper consultation with the responsible Cabinet Minister, the Defence Secretary Michael Heseltine. On or about 5 December 1985, Michael Heseltine was peremptorily summoned to Number 10, and told by Mrs Thatcher in no uncertain terms to bury his doubts about SDI, and the doubts of some of his chief advisers in the Ministry of Defence. British participation in SDI was her agreement with President Reagan, and he could like it or lump it.

Smarting with anger at the way in which he had been treated by his Prime Minister, Michael Heseltine lumped it on that occasion and issue.

The subsequent strictures which Michael Heseltine was to pile on the style in which Mrs Thatcher ran her Cabinet originated from her treatment of him over this vastly important strategic issue for East and West, rather than over the fate of a relatively small helicopter firm in the West Country."

The links between the cases of Arms to Iraq and Star Wars were brought to my attention in 1990 by former Civil Service colleagues who had shared my concerns over SDI in 1985–86, and saw similar problems developing in relations with Iraq.

The problem with Star Wars was that, as part of Britain's special relationship with the United States, including access to nuclear weapons technology, the Thatcher Government felt obliged to give public support to President Reagan's Strategic Defense Initiative. Reagan's vision was of a shield to protect the United States and participating allies from attack by intercontinental ballistic missiles, using as-yet unrealised developments of modern computer and laser technology. The British Government pledged public support, and signed the secret Memorandum of Understanding to participate, in December 1985. This was despite the fact that the project was regarded by British Ministers and their advisers as technically infeasible, contrary to the interests of industry in Britain and Europe, and liable to inflame relations with the Soviet Union.

The Strategic Trade Control section of the Pentagon, led by Assistant Secretary of Defence Richard Perle, took British participation as *carte blanche* to gain access to the full range of research that was, or could be, militarily critical with relation to SDI, and sent agents, led by the right-wing defence consultant Clarence Robinson, to visit British academic and commercial laboratories where, with my assistance, they were apprehended and deported. Secretary of Defense Caspar Weinberger visited London to apologise in March 1986. Tam Dalyell MP detailed daily events in Parliamentary speeches, which are recorded in *Hansard*.

Adherence to SDI coincided with the withdrawal of Government civil funding for research and development in advanced information technology, meaning that research funding support had to be sought from the Ministry of Defence and the Pentagon. Heseltine and Brittan had been active supporters of the Alvey Programme, and saw SDI as threatening the future development of high-technology industry in Europe. Heseltine, in response to a Parliamentary question from Chris Smith MP on 9th December 1985, conceded the linkage.

Expert scientific and technical advice was discarded in favour of adopting a policy position consistent with that of the USA, and both universities and companies were urged to participate in SDI, via a Participation Office based in Whitehall. Few contracts resulted, and Government commitment to Star Wars was only ever cosmetic, yet with highly damaging effects on civil programmes that were sacrificed, in particular the Alvey Programme.

In the case of Star Wars, there are those who argue that the deceit and pretence were justified by the subsequent collapse of the Soviet Union and the end of the Cold War. It could also be argued that it provided a critical period of political education for a community of scientists and technologists who had not previously seen their work as having a political dimension. In the 1940s it was nuclear physicists who were radicalised by their knowledge of the threat of impending disaster in their area of professional expertise; in the 1980s it was computer scientists.

IMPLICATIONS FOR BUSINESS AND BUSINESS ETHICS

When economic times are hard, it is difficult for companies to turn down lucrative contracts, and for managers to decline to follow the directions of their superiors. There is a strong temptation to leave the worrying to others, and to concentrate on the real business of making money. At Government level, for Ministers and Civil Servants, there is a tendency to focus on the good news, and to avoid public discussion of subjects that might lead to embarrassment.

Staff of Ferranti, an established British high-technology company that actively sought Star Wars contracts, and then bought International Signal and Control, supplier of cluster bombs to Iraq, experienced redundancy with the financial collapse of the company. It might have been more prudent for them to ask more questions earlier concerning their company's corporate strategy.

We face a general problem in our management culture. Technical staff feel unqualified to discuss business and political issues, or even technical issues outside their specialist field; managers feel unqualified to discuss technical and political issues; and nobody likes to admit to mistakes or even uncertainty. Modern total quality management requires people to be right first time every time, and thus discourages them from admitting if it is otherwise. The price for such deception, and self-deception, can be high.

The conclusions of the Scott Report are recommended reading.

Information Technology Consultancy

I am one, my liege,
Whom the vile blows and buffets of the world
Have so incens'd, that I am reckless what
I do to spite the world.

I another,
So weary with disasters, tugg'd with fortune,
That I would set my life on any chance,
To mend it or be rid on't.

Shakespeare, Macbeth: Murderers

Consultants have long been useful, but not always respected.

To What Extent Can Consultants Help to Prevent IT Disasters?

Experience suggests that the relationship between client and consultant may be complex, potentially exposing both technical and organisational problems. Each side may be understandably nervous, reluctant to reveal areas of weakness that may have implications beyond the current areas of concern.

THREATS

Consultants can be seen as posing a potential threat, which can be considered at a number of levels.

Who Is the Initiator of the Consultancy Project?

Was this an initiative of senior management or of the external parent company, or was the invitation issued locally?

What Is the Reason for Seeking Consultancy Input?

What is the policy brief on which the consultants are working, and is there a suspicion of ulterior motives and plans that are not being disclosed? Are the consultants under instructions to explore the option of outsourcing or otherwise reducing head-count?

Pascale and Athos [1981] note that:

> *"Most consultants will confirm that they have been called in to solve a client's problem only to discover in the course of conducting interviews that someone in the client organisation already had the solution. But because communication channels were blocked, or, more often, because the individual with the good idea was 'turned off' and convinced that the organisation wouldn't listen, no initiative was taken. The potential initiator hesitated to invest himself, in the last analysis because trying is linked to caring and history had taught him that the firm was not worth caring that much about."* (p. 145)

How Was the Choice of External Consultants Made?

All too often the major consultancy firms are preferred, as they are seen to be a safe choice. "Independent consultants" may simply be professionals between employers.

What Are the Terms of the Consultancy Brief?

Will the consultants go further than making recommendations, or will executive action be in the hands of local management? Does the work involve cooperation with local management, or is it to be done in isolation? Is it part of some wider programme?

What Is the Reporting Point in the Management Hierarchy?

Is it at corporate or functional level? What are the implications for current staff of the organisation? Are internal power structures and balances distorted?

Who Are the Recipients of the Final Report?

Will it be read first by line managers or at Board level? Will it be taken as the basis of corporate policy, or merely as a stimulus to debate? Is the report being written, at length, as an alternative to action, but as a means of placating outside bodies?

What Is the Extent of Authorised Access?

Is the approach supportive of current management structures? Are staff required to cooperate? What kinds of assurances are required and given regarding confidentiality?

What Prior Commitments Have Been Made to Action on the Recommendations?

Does this constitute abdication of management responsibility? Who was consulted, and who was by-passed? Who will have a chance to influence decisions after the recommendations are published?

How Are Authority and Confidence Undermined?

What does the process reveal about where power really lies in the organisation? Does the official organisational structure tell the whole story?

Pascale and Athos [1981] point to a lack of trust in western organisations:

> *"Employment involves a psychological contract as well as a contract involving the exchange of labour for capital. In many western organisations, that psychological contract, while never explicit, often assumes little trust by either party in the other. If the only basis for the relation of company and employee is an instrumental one, it should not be surprising that many people in our organisations do what they must do to get their paycheck but little more."* (p. 145)

SCAPEGOATS

Consultants are obvious candidates for the role of scapegoat when things go wrong. They may be seen as having only a short-term commitment, leaving the premises following their report and payment. Their perceived status and authority is in question, as they operate outside the hierarchy. They are licensed to voice what may be seen as uncomfortable truths. Their presence and recommendations may be linked to planned internal restructuring. They may be denied access to critical information; this may be deliberate, in order to invalidate their conclusions if they prove unsatisfactory. They may be countered with alternative views and policies.

There may be painful financial consequences of their recommendations, and it may be unhelpful for blame to rest on continuing managers.

SUBSTITUTES

Consultants may be used to substitute for local management decisions, enabling managers to evade what should be their responsibilities. Managers may lose ownership of problems in their areas of responsibility. They may be required to accept external intervention, despite erosion of their own roles.

Consultancy teams can disrupt information and control flow, during and subsequent to their visits. Consultancy exercises can be used as reasons for freezing local decision processes. Erosion of span of control can be tantamount to emasculation and loss of face.

DEVELOPERS

Consultants may have a developmental role, leaving local managers better able to cope. Managers can be closely involved in the consultancy process. The process can include the empowerment of managers to address problems uncovered. Consultants may conduct the work so as to plan their own withdrawal. Ongoing support may be provided on request, as part of the arrangement.

OWNERS

The issue of ownership must be addressed at the outset of the relationship: Who is to own the conclusions? Once confidentiality is broken, it cannot be restored. The mode of publication is important: Will there be a public document, or will circulation be strictly controlled? Where does the power lie during the processes of consultation and discussion?

AGENTS

The consultancy activity should be intended to lead to action, and responsibilities will need to be assigned. This may be within existing structures, or through a more radical process of restructuring and new appointments. There may be a policy decision to continue with the retention of consultants, which will have an overall impact on budget allocations.

INTERNAL OR MUTUAL CONSULTANCY

It may be sensible for one part of an organisation to provide consultancy services for another, or for this to operate on a reciprocal basis. This provides a test of internal relationships, and requires a clear set of prior assumptions, if the process is not to become confused. There may be dangers if consultants are not fully separate from the problems under consideration, if there are aspirations to objectivity and detachment. On the other hand, internal or mutual consultancy can be an effective means of developing the wider organisation, and training individual managers.

Consultants, Outsourcing and the Fear of IT Disasters

The increasing complexity of IT has come as a blessing to management consultants, who have simply incorporated IT into the range of services that they offer commercial clients.

Just as the spread of AIDS has been accompanied by campaigns for safe sex, so computer viruses have been used to stress the case for what Harold Thimbleby has called "safe hex" [Thimbleby 1990]. Detailed taxonomies of viruses have been published, emphasising the point that non-specialists could never know that their systems were free of viruses, as, like household cleaners, virus killers are only guaranteed effective against known viruses.

One approach to safe sex is to add a protective layer between yourself and your sexual partner: typically a latex device known as a condom or, to Barbara Cartland, a French letter. For corporate safe hex, the recommendation is to use consultants: don't have hex yourself, but subcontract the hexual act to outside professionals.

What is not asked is how this hex is safer when performed by consultants. The client pays for security, for not having to take the consequences of personal hexual activity. The consultants, once they have taken on the outsourcing role for the IT functions of an organisation, will decline to reveal details of any problems they encounter, and will be dissociated from the consequences of system deficiencies in the wider operations of the client organisation. With corporate downsizing and pressure to reduce head-count, the pressure on IT functions is increased, and it becomes increasingly difficult to maintain the necessary set of skills in-house.

Corporate service management have become aware of the complexity of IT systems and, rather than rising to the challenge of understanding aspects of that complexity as part of their modern management role, have preferred to delegate the concern to others. The view has been that to bring in outside consultants is safer than to trust one's own judgement. Nobody ever got fired, they believe, for buying Price Waterhouse, Touche Ross or KPMG Peat Marwick. This leaves the management consultants, extensions of the major accountancy firms, in the same position of esteem and orthodox power as was formerly occupied by IBM. Indeed, IBM are now seeking to rebadge themselves as management consultants, distancing themselves from the sale of hardware, which has achieved the status of a commodity.

IT disasters have been influential through the fear that they have stimulated among potential victims. Like horror films with the sale of handkerchiefs and the ambitions of amorous cinema back-row suitors, IT disasters have been good friends to the consultancy business:

"You are worried, you have good cause to be worried, let me hold your hand ..."

It is not clear that corporate senior management have understood what they have been doing. Given that information is increasingly the lifeblood of the organisation, and that appropriate deployment of information technology can be critical to the future direction of the business, it may be considered fool-hardy at the very least to abdicate responsibility, and give control of this crucial function to an external organisation. In sexual terms it is equivalent to hiring a gigolo to service your wife; the relationship may be easier to initiate than to terminate.

Terminating the outsourcing contract could be the most difficult part of the process. At the end of the contract, the outsourcing organisation has the option either to renew the contract with the current supplier or to negotiate a new contract with a different supplier. There is a risk that the current supplier may have the outsourcing organisation "over a barrel", since the alternative of negotiating with a new supplier could cause a costly and disruptive change-over. This is because the nature of what is to be outsourced at this point may have changed so much that the outsourcing organisation may not be fully informed about its status, thus being hampered in arriving at an informed negotiating position.

For example, parts of what is to be re-outsourced may have become integrated with another system of the supplier's as a result of the supplier's own IT strategy. Furthermore, the equipment and/or staff may no longer be the same, and assignment arrangements may not have been adequately addressed to facilitate transfer. All this could make the re-outsourcing exercise so much harder to negotiate and, ultimately, less attractive.

British Aerospace have recently moved from a prime contracting role in advanced technology projects with external clients, and quietly subcontracted their entire IT function to CSC, closely following the sale of Rover to BMW and the breakdown of relationships with Honda. This may be described as part of business process re-engineering, but it could look like euthanasia at the expense of the workforce.

The rights of the workforce are in theory protected under European and British legislation on the Transfer of Undertakings (Protection of Employment) but to date have been honoured in the breach rather than the observance, particularly in organisations without active trade unions.

It is worth following through the market aspects of this series of transactions. The financial analysts may applaud the decisions in the short term because they share both the technical ignorance and the feeling that big is beautiful. Their forecasts tend to be only reliable in retrospect; their understanding of the complexity of business and its supporting technology must be in doubt.

Understandably the failings of the major accountancy firms and consultants are not paraded before our eyes, but the courts face numerous malpractice and damages suits between the firms, who have been involved in the major scandals and business collapses in recent years, as auditors and consultants.

Accountability and Responsibility

Accountability is not just about accounts and accountants. "Being held to account" assumes a structure of law, professional ethics and responsibility, yet, in an environment of subcontracting, consultancy, outsourcing and privatisation, it is far from clear where "the buck stops".

The tradition is that Ministers are responsible for all that goes on in their Departments, and accountable to Parliament. Managers are responsible for the work of their subordinates, and accountable to senior management and, through them, the shareholders. The role of managers, and their mode of accountability, may be changed if skilled employees are replaced by technology. Management itself may be dehumanised.

Göranzon [1980] explored the problem, in the case of the Swedish Social Insurance System, of professional knowledge being replaced by the use of computers:

"It seems quite unreasonable to replace the professional knowledge and sense of responsibility among employees with a detailed steering capability built into the computer."

He stressed the continuing role of personal competence of employees:

"An individual service requires competence and flexibility from the employees."

Information technology plays a critical role, in that it provides the medium in which transactions are recorded, and thus the data from which judgements can be formed. The manager remains responsible for the judgements.

If the IT function is delegated to an external consultancy, those critical data are removed from consideration, the location of management judgement may be unclear, and conventional models of accountability and responsibility collapse. Outsourcing will often be used to facilitate major "downsizing", dispensing with the services of a tier of middle managers and in-house specialists, but the implications go far wider.

Where does this leave the individual manager? If specialist functions such as IT have been outsourced, what is left to be managed? In some organisations, middle managers are an endangered species, as their functions are perceived as being taken on by others external to the organisation. Scandinavian experience, as reported by Göranzon and colleagues at the Swedish Institute for Working Life Research, is that the absence of the knowledge of key professionals can damage the organisation some years later; only part of the work of the professional may have been automated or outsourced, and the departure of the tacit knowledge may leave important gaps.

Can ignorance be an adequate defence against criticism? Is it legitimate both to claim ignorance and to claim high salaries and performance-related pay? Is it acceptable for managers to continue to be ignorant of the technical aspects of their work? How does this reflect on the structure of status and salaries in current businesses? The management consultancies are growing at the expense of the workings of major businesses. Their own accounts are not published, and their incomes as quasi civil servants, doing the work of Government, are not challenged. They are the publicly funded custodians of the modern market economy. Unaccountable, and devoid of practical responsibility, they represent a moral black hole in the economy, fuelled by terror over IT disasters.

Business Process Re-engineering

When society requires to be rebuilt, there is no use in attempting to rebuild it on the old plan.

John Stuart Mill, Essay on Coleridge

Business process re-engineering has been defined, somewhat cavalierly, as "the radical reinvention of everything", covering business processes, management systems, and more generally roles and organisations.

It involves a focus on excellence in operations: concerned with outcomes and results, not tasks; and with physical performance and execution. In particular, it means a focus on high-performance, cross-functional business processes, and a move from paper-based to IT-based operations.

It offers a major income stream to management consultants for the next decade, and client organisations will benefit from understanding the rhetoric before signing the contracts.

BPR consultants will come with a ready list of solutions to be applied to your business, following on from the focus on procedures that has characterised the first stages of the quality movement:

- Concentrate present sequential steps into a single job; reintegrate processes, going beyond the present division of labour.
- Simplify and integrate working procedures, casting tradition and previous administrative cultures aside.
- Separate value-added and administrative channels to customers.
- Outsource activities to users or third parties; develop new relationships with consultancies.
- Prune both the product line and the customer base; focus the business.
- Replace country-based with business-based operations; take advantage of communications technologies.

- Collapse "back office" activities into fewer international locations; focus on locations with lowest labour and social costs.
- Develop shared administrative, logistics and IT "platforms".
- Use integrated data and networks to allow central management of de-centralised stock.

THE THREE "R"S

CSC like to present their solutions in slogans, such as the three "R"s of re-engineering:

- Redesign   new ways of operating and managing
- Retool   new IT and communications systems
- Re-orchestrate   leading and managing change

THE ROLE OF INFORMATION TECHNOLOGY

There is a central role for IT, and in particular for integrated software packages offered by the consultancies. In each case they plead pressure of time and point to the pivotal role of new systems.

They argue that there is usually no time to write custom code. Integrated systems are a major element of re-engineered solutions, and advanced package suites offer a way to get integrated systems more quickly. Packages presuppose traditional business processes, but they can often be configured to support re-engineered solutions. The more extreme re-engineered solutions may still require bespoke developments.

The result is that the major consultancies develop large client bases running consistent software systems under their control, a critical step towards out-sourcing, which is where the financial gains are greatest.

DRIVING FORCES

Under the general heading of business process re-engineering, consultancies can then proceed to target standard critical areas within company operations:

- Time to market
- End-to-end logistics
- Total quality management
- Just-in-time manufacturing
- Delivery effectiveness
- Service differentiation
- Organisational efficiency

The common factor throughout is cost reduction. It is argued that external consultancy can produce internal savings, facilitated by the enabling software. It may also remove effective strategic control from the organisation.

Disasters, Strategy and Development

The standard "bottom line" objective of corporate strategy is to maximise value for shareholders. The assumption is that the right business decisions will lead to a growth of turnover and earnings, although this might well involve a reduction in head-count. Business units and individual managers are set targets expressed in financial terms, with regular, or almost continuous, reporting procedures.

IT disaster prevention implies a different pattern of thinking, qualitative rather than quantitative in emphasis. The consequences of IT disaster can be catastrophic, rendering useless the normal calculations in terms of probabilities. The collapse of the organisation would negate previous individual targets, and their reporting lines.

Considering IT disasters focuses reflection on the business of the organisation. Where is IT used? Can we identify whose equipment could be at risk from definable physical threats? Who is affected by malfunctions in particular areas? Can viruses spread and create havoc like cholera in a refugee camp, thriving on pollution and disorder? Who has the critical expertise that is required when things go wrong? In years past we talked of islands of technology, isolated spots of high technology amid otherwise manual or mechanical processes. By contrast, we can now identify technology-free zones, where individuals feel free to make their own decisions, exercising judgement rather than being prisoners of data. In some cases we may conclude that this freedom is an illusion, and that the managers concerned have developed a dependence on IT without being aware of the fact, and have thus lost effective control. This can happen to chief executives, committed to thinking strategically while others work at the operational level, and losing touch with the key processes of the organisation.

This sets the scene for a variant of business process re-engineering, but with the additional dimension of clarifying the locus and structure of information flow and control. Whereas the standard advice of consultants will be to out-source the IT facilities and services that are required, we see IT as inseparable from other business functions and processes; we might as well outsource memoranda, telephone conversations and speech. IT is part of the language and culture of the organisation; those who do not use it will have little role in the future.

Ways Forward 9

Prevent us, O Lord, in all our doings with thy most gracious favour, and favour us with thy continual help; that in all our works, begun, continued, and ended in thee, we may glorify thy holy Name.

Prayer Book, Collect

Education

A change of approach is needed. We need to take the individual and collective experience of business and organisations as a prime resource.

IT should not be introduced as something new and distinct from previous experience, but as a medium for communication and representation. The limits of possibility should be noted from the start: it should not be suggested that complete IT systems are available to meet the real needs of businesses and organisations. We should talk in terms of tools, not of systems.

A starting point is reflection on professional experience, taking account of the tacit knowledge of individuals and groups. This requires a preparedness to learn from mistakes, sharing and negotiating descriptions. Premature oversystematisation can in fact be disastrous, if it cannot build on an understanding of the problem to be solved.

The model of the individual problem-solver has to be transcended, for people in practice work in organisations that are typically supported by networks and groupware. Individuals need to be encouraged to seek help, and to share information, facilitated by IT.

Technology is not neutral, and such an approach would not leave business practice unchanged.

Crises will continue to occur in an uncertain world, but they do not have to become disasters. Indeed, there may be a case for exposing more crises to critical scrutiny as a regular part of education, rather than maintaining the pretence that all is well. This could constitute an updated form of crisis management.

It has been argued that the British are at their best in a crisis. Perhaps what we need are more crises, and fewer disasters. The American tradition is to assume that technology will work, and that there is no problem that is not potentially capable of solution, given the deployment of effort and resources.

The European tradition is to be suspicious of ideologies, to which they have been subjected in the past. Technology represents merely a current incarnation of ideological thinking, the assumption that the system can have all the answers in advance of the questions being framed. Europeans do not believe such things: they know of the usefulness of technology but cannot accept talk of potential infallibility.

Given the frailty of technology, a product of human design and ingenuity, it is critical to develop and maintain human capability among all current and potential users of technology. In the modern world, this means a requirement for a high level of universal education.

This education cannot be based on the traditional certainties of Western science and technology, which have been shown to be flawed and misplaced. The younger generation do not respond to certainties that they do not respect, and that they perceive as alien to the life they experience.

The game of certainty is over. We may as well be honest, and teach people to cope with ongoing uncertainty. This means, among other things, opening up the real human culture of science and technology, which is about people exploring problems in a frequently haphazard and disorganised way, but then rationalising and justifying their discoveries to fit with the seamless development of knowledge.

Once this move has been made, the concept of IT disasters is put in proper proportion. IT crises need only become disasters for those who have previously abdicated responsibility for their own individual decisions. With emancipated approaches to education, the problem diminishes.

DISASTERS AND EDUCATION

A disaster is something unexpected and inexplicable. It catches people unawares, exposes the gaps in their defences. Having struck, it leaves an aftermath of disorder, possibly with further aftershocks as new implications of the seismic disturbance come to the surface.

Education is of prime importance. A skilled workforce in a high-technology industrial economy needs to have the conceptual equipment to cope with change and complexity.

Where the emphasis has instead been on narrow vocational competence, problems may develop. Competence in undertaking conventional tasks is not enough to equip individuals for the breakdown of the tool, the process, the industry or the society in which they have been working. When disaster strikes, the least able will be the most vulnerable.

The scenario outlined above has formerly applied in particular to those in unskilled manual employment. It now extends to office workers and junior "professionals" who have joined a particular employer with a view to a long-term career, only to find that the career ladder has been removed while they were trying to climb the bottom rungs. Such people have learned to work as part of an office system, conforming with procedures that may have been ratified under BS5750. They have not been asked to consider how to operate should the system fail.

Economic Collapse and Change

Away with Systems! Away with a corrupt world! Let us breathe the air of the Enchanted island.

George Meredith (1828–1909), The Ordeal of Richard Feverel

When policies collapse in disarray, the blame has to be placed somewhere. It may be more convenient to exonerate human agents and blame IT systems. Once things have fallen apart, there will be a need to rebuild something, probably using some of the same people, as systems developers are in short supply.

The problem is that IT systems are frequently introduced at the same time as staff are dismissed. The collapse of IT systems does not mean the return of employment for such staff, but more widespread redundancies and layoffs. There is a growing population of able and experienced unemployed, the victims of systemic disintegration, often presented as IT disasters.

In this cycle of creative destruction and economic development, the destruction is of skilled employment. It is as yet unclear what will be constructed, and how it will be sustained. It will have to involve people, and they will need to know how to work together. If economic collapse continues, new means of payment and exchange may need to be found, learning from examples set in the community and voluntary sector, using the same technology but without developing such a dependence.

The new economy will need a solid foundation of shared commitment, which implies mature democratic structures enabling consent to be expressed. It will need a richer approach to ownership, which goes beyond property to include participation in collective endeavour. It will include less differentiation than in the past between the technologies used in different sectors.

Information has become the lifeblood of organisations, but at the same time a commodity, bought and sold. It can also be shared between those with shared values. In the new flattened organisations, networking becomes an essential skill, human networking aided by electronics, and reinforced by enabling finance.

This is the stuff of utopian thought.

> *Dreamer of dreams, born out of my due time,*
> *Why should I strive to set the crooked straight?*
> *Let it suffice that my murmuring rhyme*
> *Beats with light wing against the ivory gate,*
> *Telling a tale not too importunate*
> *To those who in the sleepy region stay,*
> *Lulled by the singer of an empty day.*

William Morris (1834–1896), The Earthly Paradise

THIRD-WORLD LESSONS

In contrast to Western utopias, we can learn from the daily harsh realities of the Third World. Workers and residents in the Third World become accustomed to the failure of basic services, and evolve personal and collective means of survival. Personal survival skills are required of people at all levels of society, and even the rich and powerful are not wholly immune. Households will hope to have a generator available for use in case of a power cut. Houses may still be built on semi-traditional designs to avoid reliance on continuous power, and to provide cool interior space if air conditioning fails.

The sophisticated West has lost sight of its human roots, and it can take a natural disaster such as the Californian earthquakes to reawaken basic awareness. A similar phenomenon applies in the case of IT. With escalating expectations of systems performance, and the transformation of computer hardware to commodity status, a new danger emerges. As organisations become dependent on IT, and lack the ability to fend for themselves, they become vulnerable to IT disaster.

After the disaster there can be critical changes, as organisations are reconstructed from the wreckage. Whose knowledge turns out to be critical for the survival and success of the organisation? It may be that the contributions of many executives turn out to be superfluous and dispensable. Technical knowledge may achieve new recognition, and may be found to reside in unexpected parts of the organisation. Those with expertise need support and appreciation if they are not to move on to where they are better treated.

The general message derives from Robert Baden-Powell: "Be Prepared". We need to travel with the conceptual equivalent of a Swiss Army Knife always about our person. Individuals need the flexibility to respond to new challenges, including the technical equivalents of removing stones from horses' hooves and opening bottles. Where necessary, they should be capable of lashing together a couple of staves or building a simple gate, making a bivouac from natural materials or finding their way through a strange area by night.

Learning From Political Experience

IT disasters are only a special case of disasters in general. Lessons can be learned from crisis management and disaster recovery in the wider context. It may also be that experience in the management and prevention of IT disasters may have applications elsewhere. As the use of IT spreads and becomes more strategic, more disasters take on an IT dimension.

If, however, IT disasters are simply left to the technical professionals, and dialogue with general managers is limited, transferable experience may be wasted. One purpose of this book is to broaden the frame of reference for a discussion with critical significance for all managers.

Some cases may help.

THE CHINOOK HELICOPTER CRASH ON KINTYRE, JUNE 1994

In this tragedy, 29 people, including 25 key military intelligence personnel, died when their helicopter crashed. The causes may involve mechanical problems, weather conditions or pilot error: we will never know the full story as military aircraft are not fitted with black-box flight recorders, and any details will be treated as official secrets. The impact of the accident on the Royal Ulster Constabulary and the "battle against terrorism" was, it is alleged, greater than from any terrorist attack to date.

The question is being asked: Why were so many senior people allowed to travel on the same aircraft when, for example, members of the Royal Family are normally obliged to travel separately? It must be concluded either that security planning had not considered such dangers and their impacts, or that resource constraints on the Northern Ireland authorities were such that ill-advised economies were enforced. The business of high-level meetings, even on such sensitive matters, may have become routine, so that precautions were reduced.

The presence of highly classified documents at the accident site has also caused concern. It is not known, and will never be stated publicly, what the impact is of the loss of sensitive information in addition to staff of such seniority and expertise.

We must expect that, following the accident, new guidelines and instructions will be issued regarding security and travel arrangements for critical personnel. This stable door must be seen to be closed after the horse has bolted, but there are other horses, and other stables. The security authorities will want to get it right next time, or preferably to ensure that there is no next time.

CHANGING AMERICAN PRESIDENTS AFTER DISASTERS

The assassination of John F. Kennedy in Dallas, seen on the world's television screens, remains shrouded in mystery. We will never know precisely what happened, who fired the fatal shots, as the key players are now all dead. The presidential motorcade was driving through crowded streets, and complete security was clearly impossible, despite the heavy presence of security agency professionals. Prevention of such a disaster would only have been possible through prohibition of any contact with the general public.

Recovery, however, was relatively straightforward, at least in formal terms. The American constitution lays down clear procedures regarding what is to be done in case of the death of a President in office. There have been a number of presidential assassinations in a country where the right to bear arms has been maintained under the constitution, and the Vice-President has the primary responsibility to take over under such circumstances. No matter how charismatic and powerful the individual, the office of President is seen as having continuity. Within hours the Kennedy staff were clearing their offices in the White House, and facing replacement by Johnson appointees.

The resignation of President Richard Nixon posed a further test for the disaster recovery system, as Vice-President Spiro Agnew had already resigned following corruption charges, to be replaced by Congressman Gerald Ford, leader of the Republican majority in the House of Representatives. Accordingly, when Nixon resigned he was succeeded by a Vice-President who had not been elected to that post, but whose constitutional legitimacy was not in question.

THE DEATH OF JOHN SMITH, LEADER OF THE LABOUR PARTY

John Smith was highly respected as Leader of the British Labour Party, having won election for the leadership by an overwhelming majority. His ministerial experience and parliamentary skill made him, and thus his party, credible contenders for Government.

John Smith had suffered a heart attack in the 1980s, and though he had returned to full health, with medical clearance to take on the leadership, there was always the possibility of a recurrence of heart problems. Accordingly, the Labour Party operated a full disaster recovery planning approach, always monitoring the programme and movements of the Leader so that in the case of any problems there could be a smooth switch of responsibilities to his colleagues, and in particular his long-term deputy, Margaret Beckett.

In an era when politics has been closely associated with individual personalities, it has been an important challenge to maintain continuity of principles and practice, though pressure of events may force a change of personnel. The procedures by which personnel are changed may themselves be seen as highly significant.

PENSIONS AFTER ROBERT MAXWELL

When the media tycoon and publisher Robert Maxwell was reported dead by drowning, having fallen off his yacht, the initial response was a flow of tributes to the achievements of this Czech refugee who had built a vast fortune and business empire from nothing. His two sons, Ian and Kevin, were seen as facing the challenge of taking on the management of major organisations, following an unusual apprenticeship, and they showed signs of considerable ability.

Within a few days the picture changed, and the discussion was no longer of a family disaster, but of major fraud, as evidence was unearthed that appeared to suggest that Robert Maxwell had been systematically plundering the pension funds of companies within his empire, siphoning the money through a complex network of accounts in overseas banks. Maxwell's death thus raised the question of wider responsibility for the alleged fraud, with charges levelled against his sons and business associates.

The disaster was soon further redefined when, prompted by the Maxwell case, public attention was turned to the wider field of pensions. New and highly embarrassing questions were raised about other company pension funds where the employer had declared a unilateral "pensions holiday", suspending contributions while the funds were said to be in surplus. The British Government was found to have questionable designs on the pension funds of British Rail and British Coal, which it proposed to use to assist the funding of the privatisation process. The Government's policies to encourage the development of personal pensions, with individuals opting out of the State Earnings Related Pensions Scheme (SERPS), was shown to have been financially disadvantageous to millions of low-income employees, while lining the pockets of financial services professionals. Norwich Union, a major life assurance company, suspended their entire sales force pending retraining. Many other companies face large fines for malpractice.

The debate has now broadened to cover the entire financial services sector. Maxwell is described as having exposed the weakness of current systems of regulation, which largely involved self-regulation by the industry itself, as the Government had been opposed to statutory intervention. A change of Government would almost certainly bring legislation, and this prospect is concentrating the minds of the present companies and agencies.

HISTORY AND POLITICS

Historians will not be surprised by such accounts, as they know that it can take many years for the significance of particular events to become apparent. An event that may be seen by some as a disaster may be a critical turning point for others.

Politics could be seen as the art of disaster prevention and disaster recovery. Politicians are seeking to further their strategic objectives while lacking complete knowledge of all relevant facts, and while lacking full (or, in some cases, any) control of events. Whereas consultants seek to remain detached, but paid, observers of a situation, politicians are committed to involvement, action and change.

Politicians are increasingly aware of the importance of image and perception: one way of solving a problem is to redescribe it. Dunkirk becomes not an ignominious retreat and disastrous rout, but a triumph of the British spirit. The expulsion of sterling from the European Monetary System was presented as a principled decision to strengthen the British economy and exchange rate.

INFORMATION TECHNOLOGY SYSTEMS AND IDEOLOGY

There is considerable relevance to the experience of IT managers.

Computer systems operating in real time are the technical equivalents of political ideologies, replacing individual human judgements. Computer companies contracted to manage tax and benefit systems are engaged in the practical financial applications of ideology, where the system specification is a political document.

Companies concerned with defence, long the most lucrative sector for British IT and electronic firms, are selling systems to deliver on political objectives, defences against perceived threats from alternative ideologies.

Companies supplying systems to the "reformed" National Health Service are seeking to apply the model of customers and suppliers, fund-holding and trusts to what was previously a public service.

Managers of information technology, which in effect means all managers in the modern organisation, are at the interface between the world of system and ideology, and the real world.

PREVENTING INFORMATION TECHNOLOGY DISASTERS

Preventing IT disasters is a matter of understanding the complexity of the real world, and retaining the wisdom and humility to find a human way forward. It involves an acceptance that no one person can have all the knowledge regarding the working and technology of an organisation, and a capacity to work collaboratively to mutual benefit.

There is no infallible recipe, but there is a wealth of experience on which we can draw.

A New Management Paradigm: Human-Centred Systems

Managers need a breadth of knowledge, together with a mastery of language, and of constructive ambiguity. They must accept that the world cannot be reduced to facts and rules, that change is continuous and beyond their control, and that people prefer not to take on the role of cogs in a large economic or political machine. People need to own the purposes of their actions, and share a public description of what they are doing. Creative management involves the negotiation of purposes, meanings and descriptions, both at the level of individual appraisals and through the dynamic working of the organisation.

The challenge for the future of industry and other organisations will be to provide creative environments in which people can work, with the basic infrastructure to support the overheads of innovation and cooperation. New information technology helps us to highlight the possibilities for communication, distributed processing and cooperative working, but experience suggests that a shared technology counts for little without shared presuppositions, shared objectives and shared language [Winograd and Flores 1986].

IT enhances the importance of coordinated planning across management functions, as it is all too easy to develop system incompatibilities that inhibit business effectiveness.

Experimental work in the voluntary and community sector has borne out the effectiveness of networking arrangements between individuals and groups with shared objectives [Harris 1993; Hopson 1993]. Similar conclusions have been reached for the commercial sector in work at Harvard Business School, as it is realised that networking is a critical management activity.

Nigel Horne of KPMG has argued for the importance of collaboration between users and suppliers in the next stages of IT development and application [Horne 1992]:

"The Exploitation phase has started to bring the realisation that IT is being limited by the ability to handle the scale and complexity of systems. The Competitive Weapon phase has increased that realisation. Simply defining what systems must do in a way which allows technologists to produce them with certainty is beyond the scope of present technology. The range of possible solutions to a given problem is such that specifying a solution with reasonable certainty that it can be implemented is difficult. Getting the IT right in itself is not enough. Most systems require complementary skills in their implementation to make them usable and foolproof." (p. 8)

Collaboration is no longer an optional extra, but a precondition for competitive success:

"We need collaborations between the suppliers of technology with the users of technology in order to progress the scope, complexity and range of technical solutions of present day businesses and other organisations." (p. 9)

Needless duplication of administrative and management functions can be avoided, giving more scope for creative activity. Problems remain, even in the voluntary and community sector, with the ownership and control of knowledge and information. Those who have derived income or status from their role as information providers, gatekeepers or advisers may take exception to being supplanted by technology. They may derive security from the performance of apparently mundane clerical tasks, which may involve the exercise of tacit knowledge not accessible to the computer. Issues of skills and staff development need to be addressed as an integral part of systems development.

Denning [1990] has broadened the argument for the redefinition of management by considering the implications of international computer networking:

" The driving force for these interconnections is our desire for coordinating action in business, government, research and organisations around the world. Coordination has important implications for the design of Worldnet, such as understanding the structure of the conversations by which we accomplish action, the means by which we authenticate the persons (or machines) with whom we are conversing, and the names we use to designate others in the same conversation."
(p. 1)

Computer networks are already changing our working practices, and the nature of our organisations:

" The significance of the ARPANET lies not in its technology, but in the profound alterations networking has produced in human practices. Network designers must now turn their attention to the discourses of scientific technology, business, higher education, and government that are being mixed together in the milieux of networking, and in particular the conflicts and misunderstandings that arise from the different world views of these discourses."

The shift to creative management requires change at all levels. Governments need to provide an environment that encourages companies and organisations to invest in people, research and development. Financial institutions need to take a closer interest in their clients, supporting a long-term approach to business decisions rather than short-term speculative gain [Emmott 1992]. Creative management should mean more than creative accounting [Smith 1992]. Senior management need detailed knowledge and experience of the processes they are managing, and freedom from the tyranny of the Finance Director. Middle managers need the ear of the Board and the trust of their workforce. The workforce needs to feel ownership of the overall process, and the possibility of advancement to senior positions.

What is implied is a wholesale redefinition of management. Rather than top-down direction within a large organisation, we can expect greater prominence for bottom-up and horizontal communications, both within and across organisations. The traditional division between manager and worker, designer and builder, which has developed since the Renaissance [Cooley 1977], is challenged.

Management in a creative environment is about enabling cooperation, providing opportunities for individuals to extend themselves by working with others. Often the objective will be the enhanced quality of the process of collaboration, a socially educational process, rather than the immediate short-term product. All workers benefit from being regarded as creative agents with development potential, and with choice concerning their future area of work.

Disaster Recovery Planning as Strategic Planning

The popular capitalist style of management, advocated in paperback management texts, has been to accentuate the positive, to assume continuing success and to see every problem as an opportunity. Free-market capitalism was depicted as offering prosperity for those with the right attitudes. This doctrine was fine in the years of growth, but rings hollow in recessionary periods, when the external business environment poses challenges that cannot be so easily overcome.

The cost control style of management has been to avoid failure, and to see each opportunity as a threat. Investment in projects that encountered cost and time overruns was seen as the surest way to incur loss, and the safest route to profitability in difficult times was through cost reduction. Downsizing, outsourcing and an emphasis on finance and accounting have characterised this era. Manufacturing has been seen as a high-cost, high-risk activity, whereas service provision, particularly financial services, has offered a higher short-term return on investment. The enterprise culture has been based on the avoidance of risk. Investment has often been primarily in privatised companies, where short-term profits were guaranteed, distorting perceptions of realistic returns. Large shareholdings have been held by financial institutions, whose concern has been limited to share values and dividend levels, rather than detailed involvement in the running of the organisation.

Disaster recovery planning as a central component of strategic planning is based on seeing threats as opportunities, and preparing to deal with failures as a means of underpinning success. This approach works bottom-up, with a clinical analysis of those members of the organisation whose skills and contributions are most critical for survival, and a framework allowing such people to communicate freely across the organisation.

The analytical phase, or business impact review, may be traumatic for those in senior positions whose absence turns out not to be critical to the core functions of the organisation. If the organisation could continue without them if disaster struck, maybe their presence is unnecessary. New individuals and groups with particular technical or specialist skills, such as network managers, may turn out to be harder to replace than finance directors. Flexible organisations will be able to implement staff development programmes to meet changing requirements, but some staff may resist retraining, particularly if this involves a perceived reduction in status and income.

In democratic politics, opposition parties have to plan for the eventuality of achieving power, when they will have to put to the test their plans for recovering from the disasters that they allege have been perpetrated by their predecessors. Once in power, however, it becomes progressively harder to blame all problems on a previous administration, and it is necessary to develop strategies for recovering from disasters that may have flowed from one's own decisions. Constitutions will include systems of checks and balances, but experienced politicians will know how to get round such constraints, evading responsibility when it is convenient so to do.

The challenge becomes one of social as well as individual responsibility, with an inescapable ethical dimension. Whether an organisation is motivated by profit or by social objectives, it needs a framework of constraints, which may be expressed as regulations, which delineate relationships. These can be partially modelled in the protocols of computer networks, where it is only safe and sensible to participate if you are aware of the dangers and know what to do when things go wrong.

Few organisations in the modern world now function without the use of IT, and technical advances and falling costs increase the pressure to adopt one of a finite range of IT network infrastructures. This means that experience and insights from IT disaster prevention and disaster recovery become relevant, and even critical, to the survival of organisations in all sectors. Where such experience is not available at the highest strategic levels, there is cause for concern.

Practical Next Steps

For many organisations, time is short. They have developed dependence on a technology that they do not understand, and for which they have contracted out control to others whose interests may be in conflict at a time of disaster. Senior managers come from a generation before the general use of IT, and have been happy to delegate such matters to subordinates, many of whom have since been dismissed. In the cause of cost control, investment in research, development, new technology and training has been cut back, so that organisations lack in-house expertise on the latest developments being undertaken by competitors, and have become reliant on the services of consultants and facilities managers.

Disaster recovery planning depends on understanding of the nature of threats, alternative ways of proceeding, and means of internal and external communications under pressure. It is akin to the work of wartime resistance movements, of people preparing to take control of their own lives. Rather than the "protect and survive" ethos of Civil Defence, which takes on trust the official accounts of threats and precautions, a more relevant precedent may be "protest and survive", the approach of the Peace Movement, asking awkward questions of those purporting to lead the countries of which they are citizens.

Companies may have some trepidation about the establishment of resistance groups with cells across the organisation. If they cannot survive disaster recovery planning, this may be an indication that they would not survive disaster.

References and Bibliography

Abbott R. J. 1986. *Software Development*. Chichester. Wiley.

Abelson R. P. 1973. The structure of belief systems. In Schank and Colby 1973.

ACM 1987. *Turing Award Lectures: The First Twenty Years 1966–85*. New York. Addison-Wesley.

Adair J. 1986. *Action Centred Leadership*. London. Gower.

Addis T. R. and Muir R. M. (eds) 1990. *Research and Development in Expert Systems VII*. Cambridge. Cambridge University Press.

Ainger A., Kaura R. and Ennals R. 1995. *Executive Guide to Business Success Through Human Centred Systems*. London. Springer.

Ansoff H. I. 1968. *Corporate Strategy*. New York. McGraw-Hill.

Babbage C. 1833. Letter to Edward, Duke of Somerset.

Babbage C. 1835. *On the Economy of Machinery and Manufactures*. London. Charles Knight.

Baber R. L. 1991. *Error-Free Software*. Chichester. Wiley.

Backus J. 1977. Can programming be liberated from the von Neumann style? 1977 Turing Award Lecture. In ACM 1987.

Barr A., Cohen P. R. and Feigenbaum E. A (eds) 1990. *The Handbook of Artificial Intelligence*, Vol. IV. New York. Addison-Wesley.

BCS/IEE 1989. *Undergraduate Curricula for Software Engineering*. London. IEE.

Beerel A. 1993. *Expert Systems in Business: Real World Applications*. Chichester. Ellis Horwood.

Beizer B. 1983. *Software Testing Techniques*. New York. Van Nostrand Reinhold.

Belbin M. 1982. *Effective Teams*. Henley.

Bellers J. 1696. *Proposals for Raising a Colledge of Industry of all Useful Trades and Husbandry*. London.

Bellers J. 1699. *Essays about the Poor, Manufacturers, Trade, Plantations and Immorality*. London.

Bench-Capon T. J. M. and McEnery A. M. 1989. People interact through computers not with them. *Interacting With Computers*. Vol. 1, No. 1. April.

Bessant J. and Rothwell R. 1992. Fifth generation innovation and fifth wave manufacturing. *Proc. TTI*. London.

Bibel W. 1989. The technological change of reality: opportunities and dangers. *AI & Society*. Vol. 3, No. 2.

Blackler F. and Brown C. 1985. *Current British Practices in the Evaluation of the New*

Technologies. Lancaster. ESRC.

Blanning R. 1987. The application of metaknowledge to information management. *Human Systems Management.* Vol. 7, pp. 49–57.

Boden M. 1984. Minimizing the danger of computers. *Impact 84.* London.

Boehm B. 1981. *Software Engineering Economics.* New York. Prentice-Hall.

Boehm B. 1989. *Software Risk Management.* New York. IEEE Computer Society Press.

Bott F., Coleman A., Eaton J. and Rowland D. 1991. *Professional Issues in Software Engineering.* London. Pitman.

Bowden B. V. 1953. *A Symposium on Digital Computing Machines.* London. Pitman.

Bradbury M. 1992. *Doctor Criminale.* London. Penguin.

Bradbury M. 1993. *The Modern British Novel.* London. Hamish Hamilton.

Bramer M. 1985. Expert systems: the vision and the reality. In Bramer M. (ed.). *Research and Development in Expert Systems.* Cambridge. Cambridge University Press.

Bramer M. 1987. Expert systems in Britain: progress and prospects. In Bramer M. (ed.). *Research and Development in Expert Systems III.* Cambridge. Cambridge University Press.

Brittan L. 1994. *Europe: The Europe We Need.* London. Hamish Hamilton.

Brodner P. 1990. *The Shape of Future Technology: The Anthropocentric Alternative.* London. Springer.

Brodner P. 1995. The two cultures in engineering. In Göranzon 1995.

Brooks F. 1975. *The Mythical Man Month.* New York. Addison-Wesley.

Campbell A. and Tawadey K. (eds) 1990. *Mission and Business Philosophy.* London. Butterworth-Heinemann.

Cash J. I., McFarlan F. W. and McKenney J. L. 1988. *Corporate Information Systems Management.* New York. Irwin.

CCTA 1990. *CRAMM.* London. CCTA.

Chesher M. and Kaura R. 1995. *Executive Guide to Business Electronic Communication.* London. Springer.

City of London Police 1989. *Fraudstop.* London.

Colby K. M. and Abelson R. P. 1973. Simulations of belief systems. In Schank and Colby 1973.

Collins H. M. 1987. Expert systems and the science of knowledge. In Byker W., Hughes T. and Pinch T. (eds). *The Social Construction of Technological Systems.* Cambridge, Mass. MIT Press.

Collins H. M. 1992. *Artificial Experts: Social Knowledge and Intelligent Machines.* Cambridge, Mass. MIT Press.

Cooley M. J. E. 1971. *Computer-Aided Design – Its Nature and Implications.* London. AUEW/TASS.

Cooley M. J. E. 1977. *Architect or Bee?* London. Hogarth.

Cooley M. J. E. 1989. *European Competitiveness in the 21st Century.* Brussels. FAST, EC.

Cooley M. J. E. 1990. Human centred systems. In Ennals R. (ed.). *Human Resource Development in Information Technology.* Maidenhead. Pergamon Infotech.

Corbett J. M. 1989. Automate or innervate? The role of knowledge in advanced manufacturing systems. *AI & Society.* Vol. 3, No. 3, pp. 198–208.

Corbett J. M., Rasmussen L. B. and Rauner F. 1991. *Crossing the Border: The Social and Engineering Design of Computer Integrated Manufacturing Systems.* London. Springer.

Crossman R. 1975. *The Diaries of a Cabinet Minister.* London. Hamilton and Cape.

Curtis G. 1989. *Business Information Systems.* London. Addison-Wesley.

Dahl O.-J., Dijkstra E. W. and Hoare C. A. R. 1972. *Structured Programming*. London. Academic Press.

Dalyell T. 1987. *Misrule*. London. Hamish Hamilton.

David S. M. 1987. *Future Perfect*. New York. Addison-Wesley.

Davids A. 1992. *Practical Information Engineering: The Management Challenge*. London. Pitman.

de Mared T. and Lister T. 1987. *Peopleware*. London. Dorset House.

Deming W. E. 1982. *Out of the Crisis*. Cambridge. Cambridge University Press.

Denning J. 1992. International Networking. *Commun. ACM*.

Denning P. (ed.) 1990. *Computers Under Attack*. New York. Addison-Wesley.

Dertouzos M., Solow R. M. and Lester R. K. 1989. *Made in America: Regaining the Productive Edge*. Cambridge, Mass. MIT Press.

Dewdney A. K. 1993. *The New Turing Omnibus*. New York. Freeman.

Dijkstra E. 1972. Notes on structured programming. In Dahl *et al.* 1972.

Dijkstra E. 1972. The humble programmer. 1972 Turing Award Lecture. In ACM 1987.

Dijkstra E. 1982. How do we tell truths which might hurt? *SIGPLAN ACM*.

Din A. M. (ed.) 1987. *Arms and Artificial Intelligence*. Oxford. SIPRI/Oxford University Press.

Downes V. A. and Goldsack S. J. 1982. *Programming Embedded Systems With ADA*. New York. Prentice Hall.

Dreyfus H. 1979. *What Computers Can't Do*. New York. Harper & Row.

Dreyfus H. 1987. Misrepresenting human intelligence. In Born R. (ed.). *AI: The Case Against*. New York. Croom Helm.

Dreyfus H. L. and Dreyfus S. E. 1986. Why skills cannot be represented by rules. In Sharkey N. E. (ed.). *Advances in Cognitive Science I*. Chichester. Ellis Horwood.

Dreyfus H. L. and Dreyfus S. E. 1988. Making a mind versus modelling the brain. In Graubard S. R. (ed.). *The AI Debate*. Cambridge, Mass. MIT Press.

Drucker P. 1981. *The Public Interest*. New York. Springer.

Drucker P. 1989. *The New Realities*. New York. Harper & Row.

Drummond J. and Bain B. 1994. *Managing Business Ethics*. London. Butterworth-Heinemann.

DTI 1991. *Manufacturing Intelligence*. London. HMSO.

Durham T. 1988. *Computing Horizons*. New York. Addison-Wesley.

Earl M. J. 1989. *Management Strategies for IT*. New York. Prentice-Hall.

Eason K. D. 1988. *IT and Organizational Change*. London. Taylor & Francis.

Emmott B. 1992. *Japan's Global Reach*. London. Century.

Ennals R. 1986. *Star Wars: A Question of Initiative*. Chichester. Wiley.

Ennals R. (ed.) 1987. *Artificial Intelligence State of the Art Report*. Maidenhead. Pergamon Infotech.

Ennals R. 1989. Decoupling research from military applications. In Hassell J., Kibble T. and Lewis P. (eds). *Ways Out of the Arms Race*. London. World Scientific.

Ennals R. 1991. *Artificial Intelligence and Human Institutions*. London. Springer.

Ennals R. and Gardin J.-C. (eds) 1990. *Interpretation in the Humanities: Perspectives From Artificial Intelligence*. London. British Library.

Ennals R. and Molyneux P. (eds) 1993. *Managing With Information Technology*. London. Springer.

Evans C. D., Meek B. L. and Walker R. S. (eds) 1993. *User Needs in IT Standards*. London. Butterworth-Heinemann.

Fairley R. 1985. *Software Engineering Concepts*. New York. McGraw-Hill.

Fisher J. 1994. *Information Systems Security*. London. Reed.

Friedman A. 1993. *Spider's Web: Bush, Saddam, Thatcher and the Decade of Deceit*. London. Faber.

Galbraith J. K. 1992. *The Culture of Contentment*. Boston. Houghton Mifflin.

Giarratano J. and Riley G. 1989. *Expert Systems: Principles and Programming*. London. Chapman & Hall.

Gilb T. 1988. *Principles of Software Engineering Management*. New York. Addison-Wesley.

Gilb T. and Weinberg G. M. 1977. *Humanized Input: Techniques for Reliable Keyed Input*. New York. Winthrop.

Gill K. (ed.) 1986. *Artificial Intelligence for Society*. Chichester. Wiley.

Gill K. 1993. Human centred systems: foundational concepts and traditions. In Ennals and Molyneux 1993.

Gillies A. C. 1991. *The Integration of Expert Systems Into Mainstream Software*. London. Chapman & Hall.

Gills T. 1987. *Design by Objectives*. Amsterdam. North-Holland.

Glass R. L. 1992. *Building Quality Software*. New York. Prentice-Hall.

Göranzon B. 1980. *Electronic Data Processing in the Social Insurance Offices*. Stockholm. Swedish Union of Insurance Employees.

Göranzon B. 1992. *The Practical Intellect*. London. UNESCO and Springer.

Göranzon B. (ed.) 1995. *Skill, Technology and Enlightenment: On Practical Philosophy*. Stockholm, September 1993. London. Springer.

Göranzon B. and Florin M. (eds) 1990. *Artificial Intelligence, Culture and Language: On Education and Work*. London. Springer.

Göranzon B. and Florin M. (eds) 1991. *Dialogue and Technology: Art and Knowledge*. London. Springer.

Göranzon B. and Florin M. (eds) 1992. *Skill and Education: Reflection and Experience*. London. Springer.

Göranzon B. and Josefson I. (eds) 1988. *Knowledge, Skill and Artificial Intelligence*. London. Springer.

Gries D. 1991. Calculation and discrimination: a more effective curriculum. *Commun. ACM*. Vol 34, No 3. March.

Grindley K. 1991. *Managing IT at Board Level*. London. Pitman.

Hackathorn R. D. 1993. *Enterprise Database Connectivity*. New York. Wiley.

Hall A. 1990. Seven myths of formal methods. *IEEE Software*. Sept.

Hammer M. and Champy J. 1994. *Reengineering the Corporation: A Manifesto for Business Revolution*. New York. Harper & Row.

Hampden-Turner C. and Trompenaars F. 1993. *The Seven Cultures of Capitalism*. New York. Doubleday.

Handy C. 1989. *The Age of Unreason*. London. Business Books.

Handy C. 1994. *The Empty Raincoat: Making Sense of the Future*. London. Hutchinson.

Harmon P. and Sawyer B. 1990. *Creating Expert Systems for Business and Industry*. Chichester. Wiley.

Harris K. 1993. Information technology in the community and voluntary sector. In Ennals and Molyneux 1993.

Hoare C. A. R. 1980. The emperor's old clothes. 1980 Turing Award Lecture. In ACM 1987.

Hogger C. 1984. *Introduction to Logic Programming*. London. Academic Press.

Hollicker C. 1991. *Software Review and Audit Handbook*. Chichester. Wiley.

Holt M. 1992. Control freaks leave no room for quality. *Times Education Supplement.* 28th August. London.

Holtham C. (ed.) 1992. *Executive Information Systems and Decision Support.* London. Chapman & Hall.

Hopson D. 1993. The human user interface. In Ennals and Molyneux 1993.

Horne N. 1992. User/supplier collaborations – the future structure for IT research and development. *Proc TTI.* London.

Hughes C. 1992. Neural network technology transfer. *Proc TTI.* London.

Hugo I. 1993. *Practical Open Systems.* Oxford. NCC Blackwell.

Hutchison C. 1993. Artificial intelligence in business and industry. In Ennals and Molyneux 1993.

Ingersoll 1982. *Flexible Manufacturing Systems.* London. Ingersoll Engineers.

Ives S. R. 1991. *Managing Information Networks for Competitive Advantage.* London. Reed.

Janik A. 1988. Tacit knowledge, working life, and scientific method. In Göranzon and Josefson 1988.

Jay A. 1987. *Management and Machiavelli.* London. Hutchinson.

Jenkins C. and Sherman B. 1977. *Computers and the Unions.* London. Longman.

Jones C. 1986. *Programming Productivity.* New York. McGraw-Hill.

Judd S. 1993. Hybrid managers in information technology. In Ennals and Molyneux 1993.

Kanter R. M. 1983. *The Change Masters.* London. Allen & Unwin.

Kauffels F. J. 1992. *Network Management: Problems, Standards and Strategies.* New York. Addison-Wesley.

Kaura R. and Ennals R. 1993. *Human Centred Systems: the 21st Century Paradigm.* Kingston. Kingston Business School, Kingston University.

Kay J. 1993. *Foundations of Corporate Success.* Oxford. Oxford University Press.

Kliem R. L. and Ludin I. S. 1992. *The People Side of Project Management.* London. Gower.

Knowles R. J. 1972. *How to Rob Banks Without Violence.* London. Michael Joseph.

Knuth D. 1974. Computer programming as an art. 1974 Turing Award Lecture. In ACM 1987.

Kotter J. C. 1978. *Organizational Dynamics.* New York. Addison-Wesley.

Kurzweil R. 1990. *The Age of Intelligent Machines.* Cambridge, Mass. MIT Press.

Land F. 1992. The management of change: guidelines for implementing information systems. *Proc TTI.* London.

Langsford A. and Moffett J. D. 1993. *Distributed Systems Management.* New York. Addison-Wesley.

League for Programming Freedom 1991. *Against User Interface Copyright.* New York.

Lehman M. M. 1985. Letter to staff at Imperial College.

Lehman M. M. and Belandy L. A. 1990. *Program Evolution.* London. Academic Press.

Leith P. 1990. *Formalism in AI and Computer Science.* Chichester. Ellis Horwood.

Leith P. 1991. *The Computerised Lawyer: A Guide to the Use of Computers in the Legal Profession.* London. Springer.

Lock D. 1988. *Project Management.* London. Gower.

Louw E. and Duffy N. 1992. *Managing Computer Viruses.* Oxford. Oxford University Press.

Loveridge R. and Pitt M. (eds) 1990. *The Strategic Management of Technological Innovation.* Chichester. Wiley.

Luce D. and Andrews D. 1990. *The Software Lifecycle.* London. Butterworth Heinemann.

Machiavelli N. 1513. *The Prince.* Florence.

Machiavelli N. 1523. *History of Florence.* Florence.

Mansell J. 1988. *Expert Systems and the Accreditation of Prior Learning.* London. Further Education Unit.

Martin J. and Maclure C. 1990. *CASE Is Software Automation.* Englewood Cliffs, NJ. Prentice-Hall.

Masuch M. and Warglien M. (eds) 1992. *Artificial Intelligence in Organization and Management Theory.* Amsterdam. North-Holland.

Matsushita K. 1984. *Not for Bread Alone: A Business Ethos, a Management Ethic.* Tokyo. PHP Institute.

Maude T. and Willis G. 1991. *Rapid Prototyping: The Management of Software Risk.* London. Pitman.

Meyer D. and Boone M. E. 1987. *The Information Edge.* New York. McGraw-Hill.

Minsky M. 1969. Form and content in computer science. 1969 Turing Award Lecture. In ACM 1987.

Mintzberg H. 1973. *The Nature of Managerial Work.* New York. Harper & Row.

Monk J. 1993. Presentation at *Skill, Technology and Enlightenment: On Diderot and the Third Culture.* Stockholm, September.

Monk P. 1989. *Technological Change in the Information Economy.* London. Pinter.

Mortimer A. 1993. *Information Structure Design for Databases.* London. Butterworth-Heinemann.

Moser C. 1993. *Report of the National Commission on Education.* London.

Mosley D. J. 1993. *The Handbook of MIS Application Software Testing.* New York. Prentice-Hall.

Nohria N. and Eccles R. (eds) 1992. *Networks and Organisations.* Cambridge, Mass. Harvard Business School Press.

Norman A. 1983. *Computer Insecurity.* London. Chapman & Hall.

Norris M . and Rigby P. 1992. *Software Engineering Explained.* Chichester. Wiley.

Norris M., Rigby P. and Payne M. 1993. *The Healthy Software Project.* Chichester. Wiley.

Opper S. and Fersko-Weiss H. 1992. *Technology for Teams.* New York. Van Nostrand Reinhold.

Papert S. 1980. *Mindstorms.* New York. Basic Books.

Parnas D. L. 1985. Papers for SDIO Panel. University of Victoria. 28th June.

Parnas D. L. 1990. Education for computing professionals. *IEEE Computer.* January.

Partridge D. 1986. *Artificial Intelligence: Applications in the Future of Software Engineering.* Chichester. Ellis Horwood.

Partridge D. and Wilks Y. (eds) 1990. *The Foundations of Artificial Intelligence: A Sourcebook.* Cambridge. Cambridge University Press.

Pascale R. T. and Athos A. G. 1981. *The Art of Japanese Management.* New York. Simon & Schuster.

Peter L. J. and Hull R. 1979. *The Peter Principle.* London. Souvenir Press.

Peters D. 1981. *Software Design.* New York. Yourdon.

Peters T. 1985. *Thriving on Chaos.* London. Pan.

Pfeffer N. and Coote A. 1992. *Is Quality Good for You?* London. Institute of Public Policy Research.

Plauger P. J. 1993. *Programming on Purpose: Essays on Software Design.* New York. Prentice-Hall.

Plauger P. J. 1994. *Programming on Purpose: Essays on Software Technology.* New York. Prentice-Hall.

Porter M. E. 1980. *Competitive Strategy.* New York. Free Press.

Porter M. E. 1985. *Competitive Advantage.* New York. Free Press.

Porter M. E. 1992. *The Competitive Advantage of Nations.* New York. Free Press.

Pressman R. S. 1988. *Making Software Engineering Happen.* New York. Prentice-Hall.

Reekie I. 1993. Migrating towards software reuse. In Walton and Maiden 1993.

Ritchie D. 1983. Reflections on software research. 1983 Turing Award Lecture. In ACM 1987.

Rock-Evans R. 1987. *Analysis Within the Systems Development Life Cycle.* Maidenhead. Pergamon Infotech.

Rockart J. F. 1988. *Executive Support Systems.* New York. Dow Jones-Irwin.

Rolph P. and Bartram P. 1992. *How to Choose and Use an Executive Information System.* London. Mercury.

Rosenbrock H. H. (ed.) 1989. *Designing Human-Centred Technology; A Cross-Disciplinary Project in Computer Aided Manufacturing.* London. Springer.

Rotblat J. (ed.) 1982. *Scientists, the Arms Race and Disarmament.* London. Taylor & Francis.

Royer T. C. 1993. *Software Testing Management: Life on the Critical Path.* New York. Prentice-Hall.

Schank R. and Colby K. M. (eds) 1973. *Computer Models of Thought and Language.* New York. Freeman.

Sen D. 1991. Intrapreneuring. Presentation at Kingston Business School, Kingston University, 1991.

Senge P. M. 1990. *The Fifth Discipline: The Art and Practice of the Learning Organization.* New York. Doubleday.

Serbonati L. D. 1993. *Integrating Tools for Software Development.* New York. Prentice-Hall.

Sergot M. J., Sadri F., Kowalski R. A., Kriwaczek F., Hammond P. and Cory T. 1986. The British Nationality Act as a logic program. *Commun. ACM.* Vol. 29, No. 5.

Shafer D. 1990. *Designing Intelligent Front Ends for Business Software.* Chichester. Wiley.

Sharp A. 1993. *Software Quality and Productivity.* New York. Van Nostrand Reinhold.

Sieghart P. 1976. *Privacy and Computers.* London. Latimer New Dimensions.

Smith D. J. and Wood K. B. 1989. *Engineering Software Quality.* Amsterdam. Elsevier.

Smith T. 1992. *Accounting for Growth.* London. Century.

Smithers A. 1993. *All Our Futures: Critique of Vocational Education and Training.* London. Channel 4.

Soros G. 1994. *The Alchemy of Finance.* New York. Wiley.

Strassman P. A. 1985. *Information Payoff.* New York. Free Press.

Sutcliffe A. 1993. Software reuse. In Walton and Maiden 1993.

Synott W. R. 1981. *Information Resource Management.* New York. Wiley.

Tanega J. 1996. *Executive Guide to Corporate Environmental Auditing Systems.* London. Springer. (in press).

Taylor F. W. 1911. *Principles of Scientific Management.* New York. Harper & Row.

Thimbleby H. 1990. *Computer Viruses.* University of Stirling.

Thimbleby H. 1991. Can anyone work the video? *New Scientist.* 23rd February.

Thurbin P. 1994. *Implementing the Learning Organisation.* London. Pitman.

Turing A. 1947. Lecture to London Mathematical Society.

Turing A. 1950. Computing machinery and intelligence. *Mind.* October.

TV Choice Video 1993. *In Search of Competence.* London.

Umar A. 1993. *Distributed Computing: A Practical Synthesis.* New York. Prentice-Hall.

Veryard R. 1991. *The Economics of Information and Systems Software.* London.

Butterworth-Heinemann.

von Tassel D. 1972. *Computer Security Management.* New York. Prentice-Hall.

von Wright G. H. 1970. Explanation and understanding. Tarner Lectures, Cambridge University.

Walsham G. 1993. *Interpreting Information Systems in Organisations.* Chichester. Wiley.

Walton P. and Dettwiler M. 1993. Introduction to software reuse management. In Walton and Maiden 1993.

Walton P. and Maiden N. (eds) 1993. *Integrated Software Reuse: Management and Techniques.* London. Ashgate.

Ward J., Griffiths P. and Whitmore P. 1990. *Strategic Planning for Information Systems.* Chichester. Wiley.

Weinberg G. M. 1971. *The Psychology of Computer Programming.* New York. Van Nostrand Reinhold.

Weizenbaum J. 1966. ELIZA. *Commun. ACM.* Vol. 9, No.1, pp. 36–45, January.

Weizenbaum J. 1972. *Computer Power and Human Reason.* New York. Freeman.

Weizenbaum J. 1983. *New York Review of Books.* 27th October.

Wiig K. 1990. *Expert Systems: A Manager's Guide.* Geneva. International Labour Office.

Winograd T. and Flores F. 1986. *Understanding Computers and Cognition.* London. Addison-Wesley.

Wintour G. 1989. The rise and fall of Fleet Street. *The Guardian.* 4th September.

Wirth N. 1984. From programming language design to computer construction. 1984 Turing Award Lecture. In ACM 1987.

Wiseman C. 1985. *Strategy and Computers.* New York. Dow Jones-Irwin.

Wittgenstein L. 1953. *Philosophical Investigations.* Oxford. Blackwell.

Wittgenstein L. 1974. *Philosophical Grammar.* Oxford. Blackwell.

Woodward B. and Bernstein C. 1974. *All the President's Men.* New York. Quartet.

Wysocki R. K. and Young J. 1990. *Information Systems: Management Principles in Action.* Chichester. Wiley.

Youll D. 1990. *Making Software Development Visible.* Chichester. Wiley.

Young D. 1990. *The Enterprise Years.* London. Headline.

Yourdon E. 1993. *Decline and Fall of the American Programmer.* New York. Prentice-Hall.

Yourdon Inc. 1993. *Yourdon Systems Method: Model-Driven Systems Development.* New York. Prentice-Hall.

Name Index

Subject Index